Twenty + One

21 Short Stories

SERIES IV

"Unveiling Wisdom: Inspiring Quotes to Spark Your Life. A Treasury of Inspiration for Cultivating Positivity on Life, Love, Nature, and More."

SHREE SHAMBAV

Twenty + One
21 Short Stories - Series IV
Shree Shambav

Published by Shree Shambav, Tamil Nadu, India
Shree Shambav Ink & Imagination "Where Words Breathe and Imagination Soars"

First Edition, 2025

ISBN: 978-93-342-6397-8

Email:shreeshambav@gmail.com

Web:www.shambav.org

DEDICATION

"Isavasyam idam sarvam yat kim ca jagatyam jagat, tena tyaktena bhunjitha, ma gridhah kasyasvid dhanam"

To the Almighty,

the Divine Masters,

the family who listens,

and my parents who see –

your presence shapes the pages of my life's journey.

"Isavasyam idam sarvam yat kim ca jagatyam jagat"

Meaning: "God encompasses everything you perceive, see, or touch with your sense organs."

DISCLAIMER

The *Twenty + One* book series unfolds as a heartfelt exploration of existence, a tapestry woven with reflections on the Creator and the Creatrix—Mother Nature. Rooted in lived experiences and distilled wisdom, this work seeks not to dictate truth but to offer perspectives that may resonate, challenge, or inspire. Each realisation embraced by the reader becomes a cherished moment of insight, a seed of wisdom blooming along their own journey.

Crafted with sincerity, this book stands as an offering of love, compassion, kindness, and care—the very forces that shape and sustain life. It does not impose a singular understanding but instead invites contemplation, allowing each soul to interpret its words through the lens of personal experience.

Each story within the *Twenty + One* series serves as a testament to the beauty of life, a call to honour the delicate balance of nature, and a reminder that all beings share the right to exist in harmony within this vast and interconnected world. Through story-based wisdom, this work echoes the teachings of revered Masters who have safeguarded truth across time, traditions, and cultures.

At its core, this book seeks to impart a message of deep empathy, unity, and awareness, fostering a connection to the self, to humanity, and to the natural world. No part of its content or arrangement is intended to provoke harm, discomfort, or discord. Should any element unintentionally unsettle, it remains purely incidental and never by design.

Readers are encouraged to approach these pages with openness, understanding that the insights shared arise from a singular perspective, offered not as absolutes but as gentle invitations to reflection. These words are not directives, but guiding lights—meant to spark thought, stir the heart, and accompany each seeker on their own unfolding path.

May these stories serve as a source of warmth, wisdom, and wonder, illuminating new depths of understanding and enriching the journey of those who seek meaning within them.

Note - If any part of the book, in any sequence, hurts the reader's sentiments, it would be just out of a sheer accident, not intentional

Whispers of the Soul

21 Timeless Tales invites readers on a profound journey through life's deepest truths and emotions. Each story unravels the threads of love, loss, resilience, and transformation, blending ancient wisdom with modern insight. From the silent strength of a father's love to the forgotten dreams of a lost river, every tale resonates with universal truths. This collection is a bridge between the past and present, offering reflections that inspire and heal. These stories are not just narratives—they are echoes of the human spirit, etched with meaning and emotion. Step into this timeless realm and let your soul be stirred.

– Shree Shambav

EPIGRAM

"Stories are not merely words; they are echoes of the soul—timeless bridges between the past and the future, whispering truths that awaken wonder, kindle hope, and heal the human spirit."

– Shree Shambav

Twenty + One

21 Short Stories

SERIES IV

Shree Shambav

Shree Shambav is a 25x best-selling author renowned for his transformative works in personal development and spiritual growth.

Dear Cherished Readers

Dear Cherished Readers,

As I embark on this new literary voyage, my heart swells with profound gratitude and an overwhelming sense of connection. With deep emotion, I extend my heartfelt appreciation to each of you who has joined me on this journey.

With sincere warmth, I invite you to revisit the steps we have taken together through the pages of my earlier works. Our odyssey began with "Journey of Soul - Karma," a book that marked my first foray into the world of words and a testament to the raw passion that ignited my writing adventure.

The next chapters of our shared journey came to life through the enchanting tapestry of the *Twenty + One* series. Each page turned was a brushstroke on the canvas of our imaginations, weaving vivid stories meant to stir emotions and leave a lasting imprint on our hearts.

And how could I ever forget the transformative path we walked together with the *Life Changing Journey*—

Inspirational Quotes Series? Day by day, quote by quote, we immersed ourselves in reflections that uplifted, inspired, and offered a beacon of light to our souls, guiding us through the ever-unfolding journey of life.

The release of "Death - Light of Life and the Shadow of Death" promises to shed new light on the timeless mystery of death. Similarly, "Unleashing the Incredible Potential of Programming with Python - Optimum - PYTHON: Ultimate Guide for Beginners Series I" is poised to empower readers with newfound knowledge.

In addition, my technical book, OPTIMUM Python Series II - Exploring Data Structures and Algorithms, delves into advanced concepts in Python programming, offering a comprehensive guide for those seeking to deepen their understanding.

Shree Shambav expands his artistic repertoire with "*Whispers of Eternity: 150 Plus - A Symphony of Soulful Verses*," a heartfelt exploration of the human experience. Alongside this, his "*Whispers of the Soul: A Journey Through Haiku*" distils profound insights into poignant verses. Together, these works showcase his versatility and mastery of soulful expression, inviting readers on a journey of self-discovery. Through his poetry, he weaves a rich tapestry of emotion that resonates deeply with the heart.

Shree Shambav's latest works—*Learn to Love Yourself: A Journey of Discovering Inner Beauty and Strength Through 10 Transformative Rules, The Power of Letting Go: Embrace Freedom and Happiness, A Journey of Lasting Peace—are true treasures of self-discovery, The Entitlement Trap: Get Over It, Get On, Whispers of a Dying Soul: Unspoken Regrets and Unlived Dreams, Whispers of Silence - Unlocking Inner Power through Stillness, The Power of Words: Transforming Speech, Transforming Lives, The Art of Intentional Living: Minimalism for a Life of Purpose, Awakening the Infinite: The Power of Consciousness in Transforming Life and Beyond the Veil: A Journey Through Life After Death series.*

Each book offers profound insights into personal growth and well-being, guiding readers on a transformative journey toward inner peace and fulfilment.

In addition to these works, Shree Shambav has recently ventured into astrology with the release of Astrology Unveiled – Foundations of Ancient Wisdom Series I to VI, expanding into the realm of metaphysics. These books explore the foundational principles of Vedic astrology, offering readers a rich and practical understanding of this ancient wisdom.

Your unwavering support, enthusiasm to immerse yourself in my writings, and readiness to embark on these journeys with me have been my greatest sources of inspiration. Your input has been a beacon guiding me through the creation process, moulding these stories into containers of passion, emotion, knowledge, and resonance.

As I unveil this new narrative before you, know that your presence, insights, and shared moments have been my companions. The path we have walked together is etched in the annals of my creative evolution, and it's an honour beyond words to have you by my side once more.

Here's to the readers who have illuminated my path with their presence, who have embraced my stories with open hearts, and who have woven themselves into the very fabric of my literary world. Our journey has been a symbiotic dance of writer and reader, a harmony of souls brought together by the magic of storytelling.

With a heart brimming with appreciation and eyes glistening with anticipation, I extend my deepest gratitude for your unwavering support. Thank you for the memories, the shared emotions, and the countless hours spent in the worlds we've crafted together. As we step into this new adventure, let's continue to explore, feel, and discover the boundless horizons that words can unveil.

Warmly,

Shree Shambav

Suggested Reads

FROM BEST-SELLING AUTHOR

Endorsements

"Twenty + One – 21 Short Stories Series IV is a masterful tapestry of human experience, weaving together tales that touch the heart and challenge the mind. Each story is a universe in itself, offering profound insights into love, loss, resilience, and the beauty of transformation. This collection is not just a book; it is a treasure chest of wisdom and emotion, perfect for anyone seeking depth, reflection, and the enduring magic of storytelling."

Manju Reshma (Educationalist)

About the Author

Shree Shambav is a visionary luminary—an internationally acclaimed best-selling author, inspirational speaker, artist, philanthropist, life coach, and entrepreneur. A world record holder, his deep passion for music led him to create soul-stirring albums, drawing inspiration from his celebrated poetry collection, Whispers of Eternity. With wisdom and grace, he has transformed countless lives through his counselling, teachings, and writings, guiding individuals toward profound personal growth and self-discovery.

A 26-time best-selling author, Shree Shambav is renowned for his insightful contributions to personal development and spiritual awakening. His work continues to uplift and inspire, offering timeless wisdom that empowers individuals to embrace their true potential.

Shree Shambav's literary journey took flight with the celebrated Journey of Soul - Karma, where he delved into the depths of human experience to unveil profound insights. Garnering recognition through multiple literature awards, his repertoire includes esteemed works, such as the Twenty + One Series and the enlightening Life Changing Journey – Inspirational Quotes series.

As a distinguished alumnus of the Indian Institute of Management and the National Institute of Technology, Shree Shambav brings a wealth of corporate acumen from his tenure in multinational corporations. His most recent publications, including Unveiling the Enigma, Death - Light of Life and the Shadow of Death and Optimum - Python Series I and Series II, demonstrate his mastery of both the literary and technical spheres.

Shree Shambav expands his artistic repertoire with "*Whispers of Eternity: 150 Plus - A Symphony of Soulful Verses,*" a heartfelt exploration of the human experience. Alongside this, his "*Whispers of the Soul: A*

Journey Through Haiku" distils profound insights into poignant verses. Together, these works showcase his versatility and mastery of soulful expression, inviting readers on a journey of self-discovery. Through his poetry, he weaves a rich tapestry of emotion that resonates deeply with the heart.

Shree Shambav's latest works—*Learn to Love Yourself: A Journey of Discovering Inner Beauty and Strength Through 10 Transformative Rules, The Power of Letting Go: Embrace Freedom and Happiness, A Journey of Lasting Peace—are true treasures of self-discovery, The Entitlement Trap: Get Over It, Get On, Whispers of a Dying Soul: Unspoken Regrets and Unlived Dreams, Whispers of Silence - Unlocking Inner Power through Stillness, The Power of Words: Transforming Speech, Transforming Lives, The Art of Intentional Living: Minimalism for a Life of Purpose, Awakening the Infinite:The Power of Consciousness in Transforming Life and Beyond the Veil: A Journey Through Life After Death series.*

Each book offers profound insights into personal growth and well-being, guiding readers on a transformative journey toward inner peace and fulfilment.

In addition to these works, Shree Shambav has recently ventured into astrology with the release of Astrology Unveiled – Foundations of Ancient Wisdom Series I to VI, expanding into the realm of metaphysics. These books explore the foundational principles of Vedic astrology, offering readers a rich and practical understanding of this ancient wisdom.

Shree Shambav established the Ayur Rakshita Foundation, which is dedicated to promoting boundless growth, universal fraternity, and environmental protection. The charity helps diverse communities while working for societal progress.

To learn more about Shree Shambav and his works, visit his website at www.shambav.org. For information about the Ayur Rakshita Foundation and its initiatives, visit www.shambav-ayurrakshita.org.

Let's Follow him on Social Media: **@shreeshambav**

PREFACE

Embarking on the journey of *Twenty + One – 21 Short Stories Series IV* is an invitation to step into the timeless realm of storytelling, where the echoes of ancient wisdom and the whispers of childhood wonder intertwine. Storytelling is more than an art; it is the bridge between generations, the silver thread that weaves through the fabric of human experience, shaping our thoughts, kindling our emotions, and guiding our moral compass.

Stories have always been the silent keepers of wisdom, passed down through whispers of folklore, verses of the *Mahabharata* and *Ramayana*, and the fabled pages of fairy tales. They linger in the voices of parents and grandparents, in bedtime tales spun beneath the soft glow of a lamp, etching themselves into the depths of our hearts. These stories are not just fleeting amusements; they are foundations—shaping our beliefs, nurturing our spirits, and fostering a deep sense of belonging.

As time unfolds, these cherished tales evolve, adapting to the rhythm of modernity. Childhood companions—

Snow White, *Cinderella*, *Tarzan*, *The Jungle Book*, *Arabian Nights*—find new life in cinema, animation, and digital narratives. Though reimagined, their essence remains untouched, reminding us of the eternal nature of truth, morality, and the battle between light and shadow. Through them, children step into the shoes of heroes and sages, cultivating self-worth, courage, and the ability to dream beyond boundaries.

Yet, as we grow, responsibilities weigh upon our shoulders. The magic of childhood seems to retreat into memory, replaced by the relentless demands of life. Worry and sorrow encircle us, and detachment from pain becomes an elusive art. In these moments, stories emerge as guiding beacons—offering not just escape, but perspective. Within their folds lie not only entertainment but solutions, silent whispers of wisdom that reshape the way we see the world.

Like ancient street plays that simplified the complexities of governance and society for the common people, these stories distil profound truths into simple, accessible narratives. Their survival through the annals of history—thriving in drama, theatre, cinema, and now digital evolution—proves their undying relevance.

Fables, parables, and children's tales are more than just stepping stones to knowledge; they are vessels of timeless joy, portals to new perspectives, and echoes of our deepest emotions. To read is to rediscover—to walk through familiar paths with new eyes, to unearth forgotten wisdom, and to embrace the lessons they gently impart.

Twenty + One – 21 Short Stories Series IV presents a collection of 21 profound and inspiring tales, each an exploration of life's many dimensions. From the relentless pursuit of worldly ambitions to the sanctuary of unconditional love, from the yearning for happiness to the depths of suffering, from the enchanting beauty of nature to the resilience of kindness, from the pursuit of truth to the triumphs that define existence—each story is a mirror reflecting the human soul.

Let these tales be more than words on a page; let them awaken nostalgia, stir reflection, and reignite the childlike wonder buried within. For once, we were all wide-eyed dreamers, weaving castles in the air, unburdened by the weight of the world. Within these pages lies an invitation—to rediscover, to remember, and to relive the magic of stories, forever etched in the tapestry of the heart.

Let the journey unfold.

With gratitude and encouragement,

Shree Shambav

INTRODUCTION

Embarking on the journey of *Twenty + One – 21 Short Stories Series IV* is an invitation to step into the timeless realm of storytelling, where echoes of ancient wisdom and the whispers of childhood wonder intertwine. Storytelling is more than an art; it is the bridge between generations, the silver thread that weaves through the fabric of human experience, shaping our thoughts, kindling our emotions, and guiding our moral compass.

Stories have always been the silent keepers of wisdom, passed down through folklore, scriptures, and cherished bedtime tales. They linger in the voices of our ancestors, in the soft glow of a lamp illuminating pages filled with dreams. These narratives are not just fleeting amusements; they are foundations—shaping our beliefs, nurturing our spirits, and fostering a deep sense of belonging.

Yet, as we grow, the enchantment of childhood fades into the shadows of responsibility. The magic of wonder retreats, replaced by the relentless demands of life. Worry and sorrow encircle us, and detachment from pain becomes an elusive art. In these moments, stories emerge as guiding beacons—offering not just escape, but clarity. Within their folds lie not only entertainment but also profound insights, silent whispers of wisdom that reshape the way we see the world.

Like the ancient street plays that once simplified the complexities of governance and human nature for the common people, stories distill profound truths into simple, accessible narratives. They survive the test of time—thriving in drama, theatre, cinema, and now, in the digital age—proving their undying relevance.

This collection, *Twenty + One – 21 Short Stories Series IV*, is a testament to that enduring power. Within these pages, twenty-one tales await, each offering a profound exploration of life's many dimensions—love and loss, resilience and redemption, perception and truth, the fragility of human relationships, and the boundless strength of the soul. These stories are not mere words on paper; they are reflections of the human journey, each holding a mirror to the complexities of our emotions and experiences.

From the echoes of resilience to the silent cries of an empty soul, each story carries its own heartbeat, its own lesson, and its own whisper of wisdom. The tales unfold as follows:

- *Echoes of Resilience* – A testament to the unbreakable human spirit.

- *Navigating Life's Vast Expanse* – A journey through choices, fate, and free will.
- *Journey of Resilience* – The triumph of perseverance against all odds.
- *Embracing Self-Transformation* – The awakening of inner strength and wisdom.
- *Beneath the Veil of Prayer* – The unseen forces that shape our destinies.
- *A Call to Restore Harmony* – The delicate balance between nature and humanity.
- *Unveiling the Depths of Parental Love* – The sacrifices, the devotion, and the heartbreak.
- *Embracing Wisdom* – The lessons that life whispers to those willing to listen.
- *Eternal Bonds* – Love that transcends time, space, and circumstance.
- *Embracing Change* – The beauty and pain of transformation.
- *A Father's Love* – The silent strength behind a parent's devotion.
- *The Window of Perception* – How reality shifts when seen through different eyes.
- *The Eyes That Never Cried* – A tale of endurance and unspoken sorrow.

- *Beyond Appearances* – A reminder that truth often hides beneath the surface.
- *The Infinite Reservoir of Love* – The boundless capacity of the human heart.
- *The Lost River* – A metaphor for forgotten dreams and second chances.
- *The Tender Heart* – The courage it takes to remain soft in a hardened world.
- *Beneath the Whispering Willow* – A conversation between the past and the present.
- *The Unheard Symphony* – A melody of longing, connection, and destiny.
- *The Forgotten Roots* – A journey to rediscover heritage and identity.

Let these stories rekindle the wonder within you. Let them remind you of forgotten lessons, stir your soul, and awaken emotions long buried beneath the weight of time. For once, we were all wide-eyed dreamers, weaving castles in the air, unburdened by the world. Within these pages lies an invitation—to rediscover, to remember, and to relive the magic of stories, forever etched in the tapestry of the heart.

With love and gratitude,

Shree Shambav

PROLOGUE

The essence of *Twenty + One – 21 Short Stories Series IV* lies in its exploration of the human experience. Each story is a window into the depths of the soul—capturing the resilience of the human spirit, the delicate beauty of love, the shadows of loss, and the triumph of hope. Within these pages, the reader will journey through diverse landscapes of emotion and thought, where every turn of the page unravels a new dimension of life's intricate design.

These stories are whispers of lives lived, of hearts broken and mended, of sacrifices made in silence, and of victories celebrated in solitude. They speak of a father's unwavering love, of a child's innocent faith, of an old woman waiting on temple steps for a son who never returned. They remind us that beneath the facade of everyday existence, there lies an ocean of untold narratives—each bearing the weight of its own truth.

Some stories will embrace you like an old friend, wrapping you in nostalgia, reminding you of long-lost moments. Others will challenge your perspectives, compelling you to look beyond the obvious, to seek wisdom in the unseen. And then there are those who will simply ask you to pause—to feel, to reflect, and to surrender to the beauty of a fleeting moment.

The human heart is a tapestry woven with threads of longing, hope, despair, and joy. This collection of stories seeks to capture that essence, to resonate with the silent yearnings hidden in the recesses of the soul. Each tale is an offering, a candle lit in the darkness, a testament to the enduring power of words to heal, inspire, and transform.

Let these tales be more than just words on a page; let them awaken nostalgia, stir reflection, and reignite the childlike wonder buried within. For once, we were all wide-eyed dreamers, weaving castles in the air, unburdened by the weight of the world. Within these pages lies an invitation—to rediscover, to remember, and to relive the magic of stories, forever etched in the tapestry of the heart.

With hope and love,

Shree Shambav

CONTENTS

Echoes of Resilience

"Amidst the fleeting fortunes of life, we find solace in the enduring bonds of loyalty and love, for in the ruins of our grandest aspirations, it is the steadfast companionship of kindred souls that sustains us through the tumultuous journey of existence."

- *Shree Shambav*

In the sacred city of Kanchipuram, nestled amidst the serene beauty of nature, devotees gathered at the break of dawn to partake in a discourse led by Shree Shambav, a revered spiritual teacher. As the golden rays of the morning sun illuminated the lush surroundings, the air was filled with a profound sense of tranquillity and reverence.

Against the backdrop of ancient temples and verdant landscapes, Shree Shambav spoke with eloquence, his words resonating deeply with the hearts of his followers. He shared insights into the eternal truths of existence, guiding his devotees on a journey of self-discovery and spiritual awakening.

Amidst the gentle rustle of leaves and the melodious chirping of birds, the devotees listened intently, their hearts open to the profound teachings unfolding before them.

Shree Shambav began, "Nothing lasts forever. So....Remember... When you're up there?"

Akshay, one of the devotees, interjected, "Nothing lasts forever…"

Shree Shambav nodded solemnly and continued, "Yes, let me narrate a story. In the bustling city of Metropolis, there lived a man named Alexander. He was a titan of industry, a mogul in the world of finance, and a symbol of power and success. With his vast wealth, he built towering skyscrapers that pierced the clouds and commanded the skyline.

His influence extended far and wide, and he was revered by many as a paragon of prosperity."

Shree Shambav paused, his gaze distant as he recalled the tale. "But fate is a capricious mistress, and no one is immune to her whims. One fateful day, disaster struck. A financial crisis swept through the city like a tempest, leaving devastation in its wake. Alexander's empire crumbled before his eyes, his wealth evaporating like sand slipping through his fingers. Overnight, he went from being a titan of industry to a mere mortal, stripped of his power and influence."

He continued, "As the dust settled and reality set in, Alexander found himself alone in the ruins of his once-glorious empire. The friends and allies who had once clamoured to be in his presence were nowhere to be found. They had vanished like ghosts in the night, leaving him to face his downfall alone."

Shree Shambav's voice softened with empathy as he recounted, "Desperate and destitute, Alexander turned to those he had once considered beneath him. He sought solace in the company of old friends and forgotten allies, realising too late the true value of their loyalty and support."

"But for many," he added, "the damage had been done. They had moved on, their allegiance swayed by the shifting tides of fortune."

"In his darkest hour," Shree Shambav continued, "Alexander reflected on the lessons he had learned. He realised that true wealth was not measured in gold or silver, but in the relationships, we forge and the bonds we share. He understood that power and prestige were fleeting, mere illusions that crumbled in the face of adversity."

He concluded, "As he stood amidst the wreckage of his former life, Alexander's gaze fell upon Eleanor, who stood by his side, unwavering in her love and devotion. In her eyes, he saw a reflection of his own resilience, a reminder that even in the darkest of times, there was still hope."

"Listen closely, Akshay," Shree Shambav began, his voice carrying the weight of years of wisdom. "In the grand theatre of life, when you're at the pinnacle of success, surrounded by admirers and well-wishers, it's easy to believe that the world is at your feet. People flock to you, eager to bask in the glow of your achievements, eager to ride the wave of your influence. But beware, my friend, for in the corridors of power, friendships are often as fickle as the wind."

Akshay nodded, his brow furrowed in contemplation as he absorbed Shree Shambav's words. It was a lesson he had learned the hard way, through bitter experience and shattered illusions.

Shree Shambav said, "Amidst the fleeting fortunes of life, we find solace in the enduring bonds of loyalty and love, for in the ruins of our grandest aspirations, it is the steadfast companionship of kindred souls that sustains us through the tumultuous journey of existence."

"Imagine, if you will, a bustling marketplace," Shree Shambav continued, painting a vivid picture with his words. "A merchant sets up his stall, offering the finest wares to passersby. Attracted by the promise of riches, crowds' throng around him, eager to strike a bargain. In that moment, he is the centre of attention, the master of his domain."

"But what happens," Shree Shambav asked, his gaze piercing through Akshay's facade, "when the tides of fortune turn, and the merchant's goods lose their appeal? When his stall stands empty, and the crowds move on to the next shiny distraction? Will those fair-weather friends linger by his side, offering solace in his hour of need?"

Akshay's mind raced with memories of his own rise and fall, the highs of success and the lows of betrayal. He recalled the faces of those who had once clamoured for his attention, only to vanish when the going got tough. It was a bitter pill to swallow, but one that had taught him the true value of loyalty and friendship.

"And so, my dear Akshay," Shree Shambav concluded, his voice tinged with solemnity, "remember this: nothing lasts forever. Fame, fortune, power – they are but fleeting illusions, here one moment and gone the next. But amidst the ebb and flow of life, there are those who stand by us through thick and thin, unwavering in their support and steadfast in their love. Cherish them, Akshay, for they are the true treasures of this world."

Navigating Life's Vast Expanse

"Much like the gentle tide that caresses the shore, the love and wisdom of those who walked before us envelop us in a tender embrace, guiding us through the vast expanse of existence. In their words and deeds, we discover echoes of our own quest for meaning and purpose, a reminder that we are never truly alone on this intricate journey called life."

- *Shree Shambav*

During his discourse, Shree Shambav's said, "We often spend lifetimes in pursuit of meaning and purpose, yet fail to realise that what we seek is often right in front of us. Happiness, love, affection, and peace—they encompass us, yet we remain blind to their presence."

Bhavin, his voice heavy with longing and years of seeking, interjected, "Guruji, for years I have traversed mountains, deserts, and oceans in search of the supreme. In the whispers of the wind, the flow of rivers, the brilliance of the sun, and the shimmer of stars, I have sought His presence. "

"And have you found him?" Shree Shambav inquired gently.

"No, Guruji. I have not," Bhavin confessed, his spirit heavy with the weight of his unfulfilled quest.

Turning the conversation with a smile tinged with enigmatic wisdom, Shree Shambav began to weave a tale, painting a vivid picture of a serene sunset scene. "As the sun dipped below the horizon, casting a golden glow upon the sandy shore, two children played amidst the gentle lapping of the waves. Their laughter echoed in the salty air, mingling with the song of the sea."

Amidst their innocent chatter, a young fish named Angel listened intently, her heart stirred by the tales of adventure and wonder that danced upon the ocean's surface. With each word spoken, her curiosity blossomed like a fragile flower, yearning to explore the vast expanse that lay beyond.

But Angel's dreams were anchored to the shore, tethered by the watchful gaze of her mother, Dory. As the evening wore on, Angel's anticipation grew, her eyes scanning the horizon for a glimpse of her mother's return.

Finally, as the stars began to twinkle in the velvet sky, Dory emerged from the depths, her scales shimmering in the moonlight. With a rush of excitement, Angel rushed to her side, her heart pounding with anticipation.

"Mother, please," Angel pleaded, her voice trembling with excitement. "Take me to the ocean. I want to see it for myself."

Dory's laughter bubbled forth like the waves crashing upon the shore, a melodic symphony of maternal affection. "Oh, my dear Angel," she said, her voice tender with love. "You, your siblings, and I—all of us were born in this ocean. It is our home, our sanctuary, our very essence."

"But, Mother," Angel persisted, her eyes wide with longing, "this is just water. What I'm seeking is the Ocean."

Dora smiled softly, a flicker of understanding in her eyes. "My child, this is Ocean."

Angel's disappointment was palpable as Dora swam away, leaving her to ponder her words. She searched elsewhere, questioning other sea creatures in her quest for understanding, but found no satisfactory answers.

Observing Angel's restlessness, Dora's heart swelled with empathy. With a gentle yet firm voice, she called out, "Angel, stop searching, you little fish. There isn't anything to look for. All you have to do is look around at the beauty that exists, and look within."

As Angel's eyes widened with realisation, Dory continued, her voice tinged with wisdom born of a lifetime spent beneath the waves. "We often fail to appreciate the treasures that surround us, my child," she explained. "It is only when we face the prospect of losing them that we truly understand their value. Cherish the ocean, Angel, for it is not just a place—it is a part of who we are, a testament to the interconnectedness of all life."

And as the night unfolded around them, Angel clung to her mother's side, her heart filled with gratitude for the boundless love and wisdom that flowed between them, like the eternal currents of the sea.

With a gaze that seemed to pierce the depths of Bhavin's soul, Shree Shambav posed the poignant question, "Bhavin, what purpose, meaning, or goals are you searching for in your life?"

As Bhavin pondered the question, Shree Shambav's presence enveloped him like a comforting embrace, urging him to delve deep into the recesses of his heart.

"And what do you appreciate most in your life right now?" Shree Shambav's inquiry cut through the silence, prompting Bhavin to reflect on the blessings that adorned his existence.

"Bhavin," Shree Shambav's voice resonated with a depth that seemed to transcend time itself, "imagine the river flowing gracefully into the vast embrace of the ocean. It embarks on a journey of profound self-discovery, each ripple carrying the weight of whispered truths, echoing the essence of existence itself. In this sacred union, the river awakens to a profound realisation: it was never solitary, never separate; it was always an integral part of the ocean's majestic grandeur."

With a gentle yet compelling emphasis, Shree Shambav continued, his words weaving a tapestry of enlightenment. "Once perceived as solitary and distinct, the river unravels a revelation: it was never alone, but an inseparable fragment of the ocean's boundless expanse. This profound realisation permeates every drop, infusing them with the divine wisdom of unity."

With each word, Shree Shambav peeled back the layers of Bhavin's consciousness, revealing the profound wisdom of unity that permeates every aspect of existence.

"In the same profound manner," Shree Shambav continued, his voice resonating with reverence, "when the individual surrenders to the embrace of the higher self, a sacred metamorphosis unfolds. Ego dissolves, boundaries fade, and the soul uncovers its intrinsic oneness with the Divine."

Bhavin felt a stirring within his soul as Shree Shambav illuminated the path toward ultimate realisation. The revelation of unity, of belonging to something greater than oneself, ignited a flame of inner knowing that illuminated the darkest corners of his being.

Shree Shambav continued, "In this sacred union, solace is found. No longer adrift, but one with the ebb and flow of life's vast sea, the individual recognises themselves as a luminous thread woven into creation's fabric, pulsating with divine essence."

"As the river surrenders to the ocean's embrace," Shree Shambav concluded, his words carrying the weight of eternity, "so, too, does the individual surrender to the divine currents that guide their journey. In this surrender, they discover the profound truth of their existence — they are not mere drops in the ocean, but integral parts of its infinite majesty, forever united in the sacred dance of creation."

Journey of Resilience

"Just as the young turtle finds solace in the embrace of the ocean's guidance, so too can we discover our path by connecting with the essence of the world. Our destiny is not merely a destination but a journey of profound self-discovery and growth."

– Shree Shambav

As they walked along the tranquil coastline of Chennai, Shree Shambav and Padma found themselves immersed in the breathtaking beauty of their surroundings. The azure waters shimmered in the morning sunlight, casting a soft, golden glow upon the pristine shoreline. The gentle caress of the breeze and the rhythmic melody of crashing waves created a sense of serenity that enveloped them like a comforting embrace.

Padma's eyes lit up with wonder as she beheld the scene before her. "Wow," she exclaimed, her voice filled with awe, "the morning sun bathes the shoreline in a soft, golden glow. This place is a sanctuary of tranquillity, where nature's beauty unfolds in all its splendour."

Shree Shambav nodded in agreement, a serene smile gracing his lips. "Indeed," he replied, his voice carrying a depth of appreciation for the natural world, "this coastal expanse is a testament to the magnificence of creation, a sanctuary where the soul finds solace amidst the chaos of the world."

As they continued their leisurely stroll along the beach, Padma's gaze fell upon a majestic sea turtle making its way along the shore. "Look at that beautiful turtle," she exclaimed, her voice filled with admiration.

Shree Shambav followed Padma's gaze and smiled knowingly. "With each wave that kisses the shore and each gust of wind that whispers through the dunes," he began, his voice tinged with reverence, "the turtles embark on their journey of survival. Amidst the pristine beauty of their surroundings, they labour tirelessly to lay their precious eggs, their silent determination a testament to the resilience of life in the face of adversity."

Padma listened intently to Shree Shambav's words, feeling a deep sense of connection to the natural world around her. In that moment, amidst the beauty of the coastline and the gentle rhythm of the waves, she couldn't help but marvel at the wonder of creation and the indomitable spirit of life that persevered against all odds.

As Shree Shambav and Padma continued their walk along the tranquil coastline, Shree Shambav shared more insights about the remarkable journey of the sea turtles. His voice carried a sense of reverence as he spoke, each word infused with depth and emotion.

"The turtles lay eggs three times a year," he explained, his tone contemplative, "but never more than seven times in a lifetime. They lay up to 200 eggs at a time, a necessary survival strategy since only about one baby turtle in 1,000 survives the dogs, birds, and other predators that feed on them. It's a testament to the challenges these magnificent creatures face in their quest for survival."

As they continued their stroll, their footsteps leaving imprints in the soft sand, they came upon a cluster of glistening white balls nestled in the sand.

"See the turtle eggs," Shree Shambav remarked, gesturing towards the precious orbs. Each egg seemed to radiate with the promise of new life, a symbol of hope amidst the vast expanse of the beach.

After a moment of quiet contemplation, Shree Shambav spoke again, his voice filled with admiration for the wonders of the natural world. "The birth process of any mammal is remarkable," he mused, "and in the animal kingdom, it's shocking how everything works in unison. The turtles find the same spot, they dig a hole, and the eggs come out. It's a testament to the innate intelligence and instinctual wisdom of these creatures."

Padma listened intently to Shree Shambav's words, her eyes reflecting the same sense of wonder and fascination. "Guruji," she said softly, "the hatching of turtles is truly fascinating. It's a reminder of the beauty and complexity of life, and the interconnectedness of all living beings."

As the gentle waves lapped against the shore and the moon cast its ethereal glow upon the beach, Shree Shambav broke the silence with a deep, contemplative sigh.

"The process of sea turtles laying eggs and their subsequent hatching is a fascinating and intricate journey deeply ingrained in the natural world," he began, his voice carrying a sense of reverence for the miracle of life unfolding before them.

Padma, her eyes shining with curiosity, leaned in closer to listen. "Tell me more, Guruji," she said eagerly, her voice barely above a whisper.

Shree Shambav nodded, his gaze drifting out to sea as he spoke. "Female sea turtles return to the same beachcs where they were born to lay their eggs, a phenomenon known as natal homing," he explained. "Using their powerful flippers, they dig a deep hole in the sand, known as a nest chamber, where they deposit their eggs. The process of nesting typically occurs at night to avoid predators and excessive heat."

Padma's brow furrowed with wonder. "And what happens next?" she asked, her voice filled with anticipation.

Shree Shambav offered a knowing smile. "Once the eggs are laid, the mother turtle carefully covers the nest with sand to protect them from harm," he continued. "The eggs remain buried in the warm sand for an incubation period that typically lasts around two months, depending on the species and environmental conditions. During this time, the eggs are kept warm by the surrounding sand, providing the ideal conditions for the embryos to develop."

Padma nodded in understanding; her mind filled with images of the precious eggs nestled safely in their sandy cocoon. "But what happens when the eggs finally hatch?" she asked, her voice tinged with excitement.

Shree Shambav's eyes sparkled with anticipation as he replied, "When the time is right, the hatchlings begin to emerge from their eggs. Using a specialised structure called a caruncle, located on their snout, the hatchlings break through the eggshell and make their way to the surface of the sand. Once they reach the surface, they instinctively pause to absorb oxygen and orient themselves before beginning their journey."

As they stood on the beach, bathed in the soft, silvery light of the moon, with each delicate step taken by the newly hatched turtles, they knew that they were witnessing the timeless dance of nature, a reminder of the beauty and resilience of the world around them.

Shree Shambav's words hung in the air, a tapestry of wonder and reverence woven with threads of deep emotion and contemplation. "Padma," he began, his voice carrying the weight of ancient wisdom and profound insight, "don't you think the waves and breezing wind were a gentle lullaby for the young restless spirit who was waiting for the moment of its emergence?"

Padma listened intently, her heart stirred by the profound questions posed by her beloved Guruji. "How did the young one know to feed itself to grow stronger and more vibrant, nourished by the nutrients provided by its egg?" Shree Shambav continued, his eyes reflecting the infinite mysteries of the natural world. "And how did it realise when to emerge from the egg? Was there any guiding force, a nurturing energy that whispered words of wisdom and encouragement?"

Padma felt a sense of awe wash over her as she pondered the mysteries of life and creation. "Is it not life's greatest miracle," Shree Shambav mused, his words carrying the weight of centuries of wisdom, "that the hatchling instinctively knew it was preparing for something greater beyond its shell?"

As Padma nodded along with the other devotees, Shree Shambav's voice took on a gentle yet authoritative tone. "Under the cover of darkness," he explained, "the hatchlings emerge from the nest and make their way towards the ocean, guided by the faint glow of the horizon. They navigate using cues such as the slope of the beach, the brightness of the night sky, and the sound of the ocean waves."

Padma's heart swelled with admiration for the resilience and determination of the tiny hatchlings. "This journey is fraught with dangers," Shree Shambav continued, his voice tinged with solemnity, "as predators such as birds, crabs, and other animals lie in wait to prey on the vulnerable hatchlings."

With bated breath, Padma listened as Shree Shambav described the final, perilous leg of the hatchlings' journey. "Upon reaching the water's edge," he explained, "the hatchlings face their final challenge. They must navigate the turbulent surf and powerful waves to reach the safety of the open ocean."

Padma's heart raced with anticipation as she imagined the hatchlings braving the crashing waves with nothing but their instinct and determination to guide them. "Once the hatchlings have successfully entered the ocean," Shree Shambav concluded, his voice filled with quiet reverence, "they embark on a remarkable journey of survival, navigating vast distances and facing numerous threats along the way."

As Padma gazed out at the vast expanse of the ocean, her heart filled with admiration for the resilience and courage of the hatchlings. Though they may never physically reunite with their mother, the bond forged through the shared experience of nesting and hatching remained an integral part of their instinctual behaviour, a testament to the enduring power of life's greatest miracle.

Padma's voice trembled with concern as she voiced her question to Shree Shambav, her eyes reflecting the depths of her empathy and compassion. "Guruji, young ones will not reunite with their mother," she said, her heart heavy with sorrow at the thought of the hatchlings embarking on their perilous journey alone.

Shree Shambav's smile was a beacon of serenity amidst Padma's turmoil, his eyes twinkling with the light of wisdom as he prepared to impart his teachings. "Let me narrate a small story," he began, his voice a gentle melody that carried the promise of solace and understanding. "Once, a young turtle found itself at the crossroads of its life journey, hesitant to venture into the vast expanse of the ocean. It prayed to the supreme, asking for guidance in the face of the unknown and the diversity of dangers that lay ahead."

With a flash of light and a deafening roar, the young turtle's prayers were answered, as a wise old crab appeared before it, its presence radiating an aura of ancient wisdom and benevolence. The crab approached the turtle with a kind smile, offering words of wisdom and guidance that echoed through the depths of its soul.

"Dear turtle," the crab said, its voice a soothing balm to the turtle's troubled spirit, "you are embarking on a great adventure, but remember to trust in your instincts and follow the path laid out before you. The ocean is your home, and it will guide you to your destiny."

The turtle nodded gratefully, feeling a sense of comfort and reassurance wash over it like the gentle caress of the ocean's waves. It knew that it was not alone in its journey, that the wisdom of the ages and the love of the universe were with it every step of the way.

As the young turtle made its way towards the sea, it encountered a school of fish gliding gracefully through the water, their movements a testament to the harmony and interconnectedness of all living beings. Intrigued by their fluid motions, the turtle approached them, seeking answers to the questions that weighed heavily on its mind.

The leader of the fish regarded the turtle with a kind smile, its eyes twinkling with the light of shared understanding. "We may be small," the fish said, its voice carrying the wisdom of generations past, "but we are part of something much larger than ourselves. The ocean is our home, and it teaches us everything we need to know. Trust in its currents, and it will lead you to where you belong."

With newfound confidence and a heart filled with gratitude, the turtle dived into the water, embracing the cool embrace of the ocean as it enveloped him in its embrace. And as it swam further and further from the shore, guided by the wisdom of the sea and the love of those who had helped it along the way, the turtle knew that it was finally home, reunited with the mother nature that had always been there, silently watching over it from the depths below.

Shree Shambav's smile illuminated his face with a warmth that mirrored the golden hues of the sun setting over the horizon. "Overall," he said, his voice a gentle melody that danced on the breeze, "the process of sea turtle nesting and hatching is a testament to the resilience and adaptability of these remarkable creatures."

Padma listened intently, her heart swelling with reverence for the natural world and the wisdom it imparted. "Yes, Guruji," she replied, her voice soft with awe, "it's truly remarkable how these creatures navigate the challenges of life with such grace and determination."

Shree Shambav nodded, his eyes sparkling with the light of understanding. "The story of the young turtle," he continued, his words carrying the weight of ancient wisdom, "teaches us the importance of trusting in our instincts and following the path laid out before us."

Padma nodded in agreement, her mind buzzing with the profound significance of Shree Shambav's words. "Yes," she said, her voice filled with conviction, "just as the turtle relied on the guidance of the ocean and the wisdom of those around it, we too can find strength and direction by connecting with the world around us."

Shree Shambav's gaze softened, his eyes reflecting the boundless depths of compassion and understanding. "And in doing so," he concluded, his voice a gentle whisper that echoed through the recesses of Padma's soul, "we may discover that our true destiny lies not in seeking answers, but in embracing the journey itself."

Embracing

Self-Transformation

"Self-transformation is not a destination but a journey of awakening, where we shed old beliefs and fears, emerging as the empowered architects of our own destiny."

– Shree Shambav

In the tranquil embrace of the ashram, Shree Shambav and his devoted followers sat beside the serene riverbank, where the soft murmur of flowing water wove into the peaceful ambiance. Padma, her heart brimming with a longing for deeper understanding, gently initiated the conversation.

"Guruji," Padma began, her voice a blend of earnest curiosity and reverence, "what does self-transformation truly mean to you?"

Guruji, his eyes reflecting both serenity and profound thought, met Padma's gaze before responding with a calm certainty. "Padma, self-transformation is the pinnacle of human achievement. It's about embracing and embodying our most authentic selves."

As the conversation unfolded, Guruji's words carried a weight of wisdom honed through years of introspection and spiritual practice. "Self-transformation," he continued, "is not merely about making surface-level changes. It's a profound journey of inner refinement, where we consciously shed limiting beliefs, behaviors, and perspectives that hinder our growth."

His gaze momentarily shifted to the tranquil river flowing beside them, as if drawing inspiration from nature itself. "Through this process," Guruji elaborated, "we cultivate a deeper understanding of our true essence and align ourselves with a higher purpose—a purpose rooted in compassion, resilience, and wisdom."

He paused briefly, allowing his words to settle like ripples on the water, before continuing with a gentle intensity. "It's an ongoing evolution that encompasses every facet of our being—our physical vitality, emotional depth, mental clarity, and spiritual awakening. Self-transformation demands courage to confront our vulnerabilities, to delve into the depths of our souls with unwavering honesty."

"In essence," Guruji concluded, his voice resonating with clarity and depth, "self-transformation is the sacred journey of becoming whole, of harmonising our inner and outer selves until we radiate the authenticity of our true nature."

Padma, let me tell you a story that has always moved me deeply. It's about a small village called Arpakkam, nestled amidst lush greenery and gentle hills. This village was home to simple, hardworking people who lived their lives in harmony with nature. The air was always filled with the scent of blooming flowers, and the sound of birds singing could be heard from dawn till dusk.

One day, a monk on his long journey of spiritual exploration found his way to Arpakkam. His robes were tattered, and his eyes carried the weight of a thousand untold stories. The villagers were wary of this stranger with an unknown identity. Whispers and suspicions spread like wildfire. They gathered to discuss his fate, wanting him gone as soon as possible.

An elderly man, wise with age, stood up during the meeting and said, 'Let us give him some time to settle. If he is harmless, let him stay.' The villagers agreed, albeit reluctantly.

Days turned into weeks, and the monk began to weave himself into the fabric of the village. His knowledge, kindness, and compassion touched many hearts. People started to share their pains with him and found solace in his words. The monk's presence became a source of comfort, and his composure and gentle way of speaking won over even the most skeptical.

The monk encouraged the villagers to plant more trees, build water reservoirs, and construct high-rise water tanks around densely populated areas. 'Prepare for the unexpected,' he would say with a serene smile. Some villagers heeded his advice, planting trees and building the tanks. Others laughed, thinking it was unnecessary. 'Why do we need water tanks when we have sufficient water?' they scoffed. 'This monk is crazy, making people work for no reason.'

Curiosity grew among the villagers. They wondered where the monk travelled during the day. He would leave in the morning and return by evening, sharing his wisdom and guiding the people. Some villagers began to speculate, questioning his intentions.

One fateful evening, disaster struck. A fire broke out, spreading swiftly like a ravenous beast, consuming everything in its path. Panic ensued, and the village was engulfed in chaos. People were terrified, fearing they would lose everything they held dear. Amidst the turmoil, the monk remained calm and composed. He called out to a villager named Ram.

'Ram,' he said with a commanding yet gentle tone, 'go and open all the four water tanks.'

Ram, trusting the monk completely, did as he was told. Meanwhile, the monk urged everyone to evacuate. Though some resisted, they eventually heeded his words and fled. Water gushed out from the tanks, flooding the village and extinguishing the fire. The flames were no match for the deluge, and the village was saved.

As the night wore on, the villagers, exhausted but relieved, gathered to thank the monk. They wanted to build him a house and provide for his needs. But the next day, and the days that followed, the monk was nowhere to be found. He had vanished as mysteriously as he had appeared.

Confusion and sadness settled over Arpakkam as the villagers gathered to discuss the monk's sudden disappearance. They spoke in hushed tones, trying to make sense of his abrupt departure. Suddenly, a child interrupted, saying, "Father, I have completed my work, and I must leave now."

Everyone was bewildered by the child's statement, their confusion deepening.

A voice rang out, "It's a message." It was the voice of one of the village's staunchest skeptics. Tears streamed down his face as he laughed bitterly. "The revered monk's work here was done, and he has left. I never believed in him. I called him a liar and mocked those who followed him. But he came with a purpose, fulfilled it, and now he's gone. He has left a mark on this village that will never fade."

After a long silence, Ram, his voice trembling with emotion, spoke up, "We need to move on with the teachings he left us. He has given us an invaluable gift."

The villagers, their hearts heavy with regret, realised the depth of their loss. They gathered in small groups, whispering among themselves, their voices tinged with sorrow and longing. Some wept openly, their tears a testament to the monk's profound impact.

"We took too long to understand him," an elderly woman said, her voice breaking. "He was a beacon of wisdom and compassion, and we were too blind to see it."

"We must live by the principles he graced upon us," another villager added, wiping away his tears. "He taught us kindness, resilience, and the importance of preparation. His lessons were not just for the moment, but for a lifetime."

Ram, struggling to hold back his own tears, continued, "Yes, it haunts me how we take things for granted. Only when we lose them do we understand their true value. The monk's presence was a blessing, and his departure a reminder of the fleeting nature of life and the enduring power of his teachings."

The villagers stood in a solemn circle, each reflecting on their interactions with the monk. They remembered his gentle smile, his calming presence, and the wisdom he imparted so freely. The once skeptical man, now overwhelmed with guilt and admiration, spoke again, "He came into our lives quietly, like a gentle breeze, and left us forever changed. We owe it to him, and to ourselves, to carry forward his legacy."

In the days that followed, the village of Arpakkam began to transform. Trees were planted with renewed vigor, water reservoirs were maintained meticulously, and the high-rise water tanks stood as a testament to the monk's foresight. The villagers worked together, united by a shared sense of purpose and gratitude. The monk's teachings had become the foundation of their community, guiding them towards a future filled with hope and resilience.

The children of Arpakkam grew up hearing stories of the wise monk who had saved their village. His lessons were woven into the fabric of their lives, shaping their values and actions. The village thrived, not just because of the physical changes, but because of the spiritual and emotional growth inspired by the monk's presence.

Guruji's voice carried a blend of admiration and reflection as he concluded, "The monk's legacy in Arpakkam teaches us that true wisdom lies not in mere words but in actions that inspire transformation. His departure left a profound void, but also ignited a spirit of unity and resilience among the villagers. His teachings endure, guiding them towards a future shaped by compassion, wisdom, and the pursuit of inner truth."

Padma listened intently, her soul stirred by the profound insights Guruji shared. In his words, she found not only guidance for her own path but also a profound reminder of the transformative power inherent in embracing one's true self. The ashram, with its tranquil surroundings and the wisdom that flowed like the river beside them, became a sanctuary where Padma could embark on her own journey of self-discovery and inner growth.

As they sat by the riverbank, enveloped in the serenity of the ashram, Padma felt a deep sense of gratitude for Guruji's guidance. His teachings had illuminated a path forward—one that promised not just personal fulfillment but also a profound connection to the universal truths that underpin existence. And so, amidst the gentle murmur of flowing water and the timeless wisdom of the ashram, Padma's quest for self-transformation began—a journey destined to unfold with courage, compassion, and a steadfast commitment to living authentically.

And so, in the tranquil setting of the ashram, amidst the gentle flow of the river and the wisdom shared, Padma found herself on the threshold of a profound journey—a journey towards embracing her truest self and honouring the transformative power within.

Beneath the Veil of Prayer

"Amidst the symphony of longing hearts, woven into the fabric of the universe, we uncover the profound beauty of resilience and the transformative power of faith."

– Shree Shambav

In the tranquil city of Kanchipuram, as the sun tenderly dipped below the horizon, casting a canvas of orange and pink across the sky, the world seemed to sigh in unison, embracing the onset of night. Birds gracefully returned to their nests, their songs of the day fading into a gentle murmur, while a cool breeze whispered through the streets, urging weary souls to pause and find solace in the stillness. As nocturnal creatures stirred, preparing for their nightly rituals, the city exuded a sense of serenity that enveloped all who dwelled within it.

Amidst this serene backdrop, within the sacred space of an evening discourse, young Jun sat before his master, Shree Shambav, his heart heavy with questions that danced on the edge of his consciousness. "Master," he began, his voice trembling with a mixture of curiosity and yearning, "why must we pray? What is the true essence of prayer? And what do we truly gain from it?"

The air itself seemed to hold its breath, as if anticipating the weight of Shree Shambav's response, the echo of Jun's words lingering in the stillness of the evening.

Shree Shambav spoke with a voice rich with depth and emotion, each word carrying the weight of centuries-old wisdom. "Jun," he began, his gaze gentle yet penetrating, "prayer serves as a profound expression of connection — with ourselves, with each other, and with something greater than ourselves. It is a sacred conduit through which we acknowledge our vulnerability, our hopes, fears, and gratitude. In moments of joy, prayer becomes a melody of celebration, a heartfelt expression of gratitude for the blessings bestowed upon us. In times of sorrow or struggle, it offers solace, a comforting embrace that reminds us we are never alone in our journey."

He paused, allowing the gravity of his words to settle upon Jun's eager heart. "Moreover," Shree Shambav continued, his voice resonating with a quiet intensity, "prayer is a spiritual discipline, a practice that guides us toward mindfulness, resilience, and a deeper understanding of our place in the vast tapestry of the universe."

"The essence of prayer," Shree Shambav spoke softly, his eyes alight with ancient wisdom, "lies not in the mere recitation of words or performance of rituals, but in the sincerity of our intention. It is a sacred dialogue, a heartfelt communion with the divine, wherein we surrender our ego, our desires, and our fears, aligning ourselves with the boundless wisdom and guidance that emanates from the source of all creation."

As Shree Shambav's words wove a tapestry of enlightenment, Jun listened with rapt attention, his soul stirred by the profundity of his master's teachings.

"And now," Shree Shambav's voice took on a melodic cadence, carrying the essence of a timeless tale, "let me share with you a story — a tale that speaks to the power of prayer and the longing of the human spirit."

In the heart of the bustling city, within the confines of a lavish apartment adorned with opulence and wealth, young Alex knelt beside his bed, tears streaming down his cheeks. With a voice trembling with raw emotion, he poured out his anguish to the heavens. "Why, God?" he cried out, his words a desperate plea born from the depths of his wounded heart. "Why did you give me such terrible parents? They never buy me the toys I want; they never have time to play with me. It's not fair!"

His voice echoed off the gilded walls, reverberating with bitterness and resentment, yet beneath the anger lay a profound sense of hurt and longing that threatened to consume him.

Meanwhile, on the outskirts of the city, in a humble orphanage nestled amidst the quietude of forgotten streets, another child named Daisy gazed up at the night sky, her eyes shimmering with unshed tears. With a voice as soft as a whisper, she spoke her silent prayer into the vast expanse of the universe. "God," she murmured, her words a fragile plea that hung in the air like a delicate thread, "why am I all alone in this world? Why don't I have parents like the other kids? All I want is someone to love me, to hold me, to call me their own."

Her voice, barely audible above the distant hum of the city, carried the weight of a lifetime of longing and yearning for the warmth of a loving embrace.

As the night wore on, the city slumbered, unaware of the silent symphony of prayers that reverberated through its streets. And yet, in the quiet stillness of the night, a transformation began to unfold.

In Alex's opulent abode, a shift stirred within the depths of his soul. Amidst the trappings of material wealth, a seed of realisation took root, blossoming into a newfound understanding. In his despair, he glimpsed the fleeting nature of earthly possessions and the emptiness they left in their wake. And in that moment of clarity, he began to yearn for something deeper, something more profound than the fleeting allure of worldly riches.

Similarly, in Daisy's humble sanctuary, a gentle presence wrapped itself around her fragile form, soothing her troubled spirit with a sense of peace and comfort. In the quiet solitude of her surroundings, she felt a connection to something greater than herself, an invisible thread of love that bound her to the very fabric of existence.

In the days that followed, Alex and Daisy embarked on separate yet parallel journeys of self-discovery and transformation. Guided by the whispers of their hearts, they learned to find solace in the simple joys of life, to cherish the bonds of family and friendship that transcended the boundaries of circumstance.

Though their paths never crossed, Alex and Daisy were united by a common thread - the universal longing for love and belonging that resonated within the depths of their souls. And in their shared journey of healing and redemption, they discovered the true essence of prayer - a sacred communion with the divine that transcended the limitations of earthly existence.

As Shree Shambav spoke, his voice infused with depth and emotion, he imparted a timeless wisdom that echoed through the ages. "Jun," he said, his words a gentle reminder of the sacred power of prayer, "it is a sacred doorway through which we access the depths of our souls and commune with the divine, finding solace, strength, and wisdom along the way."

A Call to Restore Harmony

"Within the embrace of nature's symphony, we find ourselves woven into the fabric of existence, enveloped by the gentle whispers of leaves and the resounding chorus of life. Yet, in our haste, we risk overlooking the profound interconnectedness that sustains us, failing to grasp the sacredness of each fluttering wing and rustling branch."

– Shree Shambav

As Shree Shambav and his devoted followers wandered through the woods, he spoke with a voice filled with reverence and emotion. "Behold," he exclaimed, "nature's bountiful offerings envelop us in a melodic symphony of birdsong, the graceful dance of flowing rivers, and the gentle whispers of rustling leaves. With each passing breeze, fluttering butterfly, and buzzing bee, we are embraced by the fragrant essence of blooming flowers."

Seated beneath the towering canopy of ancient trees, Shree Shambav's voice resonated with depth and passion. "Here," he continued, "we find solace and sustenance, breathing in the life-affirming oxygen that sustains our existence. Yet, amidst this rich tapestry of life, we often fail to recognise the intricate web of interconnectedness that nurtures us, overlooking the sacredness of the blessings bestowed upon us. It is during moments of introspection that we must awaken to the profound significance of our bond with the natural world, honouring and safeguarding its magnificence for the prosperity of future generations."

"We should be careful," Shree Shambav cautioned, his tone tinged with concern, "while we dismantle this equilibrium. Everything, every being that exists on this earth, is dependent on each other. If we recklessly handle the ecosystem around us, we will have to face the consequences."

Akanksh pondered aloud, his voice tinged with curiosity and a hint of hesitation. "Guruji," he began, "if growth demands sacrifice, must we not relinquish certain aspects of our lives, even those dear to us, to pursue a greater cause?"

Akanksh's question prompted a thoughtful smile from Shree Shambav. "True," he replied, "but the question arises: to what extent do we have to give away?"

With a sense of urgency, Shree Shambav continued, "Have we truly understood the complexity and interconnectivity of the ecosystem? Have we grasped the impact it can have on all living beings? Let us understand a simple phenomenon of seed growth."

"Consider this," he urged, his voice compelling and full of emotion. "A tree grows in two directions - Phototropic and Gravitropic. A seed first pushes down, resisting dampness, dirt, and rooting its strong root system below the mud, along the rock, even before it emerges as green... even before it sees its first light. Once it sees light, there is no more resistance for growth. But the tree must also resist the scratching heat, the blowing wind, to become a beautiful, gigantic tree - a dwelling house for many creatures and birds, a wondrous creation of oxygen-generating machine by the Supreme. Like the tree, everybody wants to embrace the Phototropic nature and enjoy the fruit, but no one wants to see the Gravitropic behind the fruit. If you are unwilling to see the other side, then you will not see what you want to see."

Shree Shambav's voice softened, carrying a weight of sorrow as he began to narrate a story. "Let me tell you of a day when two birds were flying across meadows," he said, his words tinged with emotion. "A young bird named Chipper asked its mother, Fifi, what that sound was. Fifi replied that a dense area of trees was being chopped."

Chipper's voice trembled as he asked, "What would happen to our relatives living in those huge trees?"

Fifi's eyes welled up with tears as she replied, "They need to find new trees in adjacent areas to build their nests."

Chipper persisted, "What about the other living beings that coexist in that tree?"

Fifi's tears flowed freely now as she answered, "They would all die."

"Mother," Chipper's voice quivered, "why do they kill them all?"

With tears streaming down her cheeks, Fifi continued, "My brother, sisters, my friends are suffering due to air pollution, caused by the waste of many industries, biochemicals, and wars."

Chipper's voice cracked, "Mother, aren't they happy with the sheer beauty of this nature and its gifts?"

Fifi sighed heavily, "Child, they are consumed by greed."

"We can only pray to the Almighty," Fifi's voice wavered, "and plead with mankind to stop poisoning the air. They are not only killing all beings but also themselves, unaware. The recent disease, COVID, took many lives. I watched my siblings struggle to breathe and perish."

Tears continued to fall as Fifi recounted, "Past memories haunt me, seeing people falling like a pack of cards, paying to breathe, fighting for oxygen cylinders. It was chaos everywhere. Some struggled for food, some for shelter as trees vanished, making water scarce."

"It was a truly sad state," Fifi concluded, her voice heavy with sorrow.

Chipper, still bewildered, asked, "Even after such disaster, why do they still chop the trees?"

Fifi's voice quivered with emotion, "They are driven by greed, Chipper. They take nature for granted, only interested in material gain, ignoring the existence of other beings in the ecosystem. Humans can only thrive in diversity, otherwise, they must pay for their actions against nature."

Shree Shambav's voice then shifted, resonating with a mixture of empathy and urgency. "The recent crises, such as the devastating COVID-19 pandemic and the relentless onslaught of natural disasters, serve as poignant reminders of our profound vulnerability in the face of nature's wrath. By neglecting the delicate balance of ecosystems, we have unwittingly paved the path to disaster, inviting chaos and calamity to wreak havoc upon our lives."

Consider, for instance, the catastrophic impact of deforestation in regions prone to landslides and floods. The loss of vital forest cover not only disrupts local ecosystems but also leaves communities exposed to heightened risks of natural disasters. The tragic consequences are all too real, with lives lost, homes destroyed, and livelihoods shattered in the wake of such environmental degradation.

Shree Shambav's voice took on a somber tone as he addressed Akanksh. "Similarly, the unchecked pollution of our air, water, and soil has dire implications for public health," he said, his words heavy with concern. "From respiratory ailments caused by air pollution to waterborne diseases stemming from contaminated water sources, the repercussions of environmental negligence are far-reaching and devastating."

He paused, allowing the weight of his words to sink in before continuing. "Moreover, the mental toll of ecological imbalance cannot be overstated. As communities grapple with the aftermath of environmental disasters, the psychological impact is profound," his voice tinged with empathy. "It leads to increased stress, anxiety, and trauma. The erosion of natural habitats also robs individuals of the solace and rejuvenation that nature provides, further exacerbating mental health challenges."

"In the face of these hardships," Shree Shambav's voice grew more urgent, "it becomes increasingly apparent that our well-being is intricately linked to the health of the planet. Our disregard for the environment not only imperils ecosystems and biodiversity but also threatens the very foundation of human existence."

He sighed heavily, his voice laced with a mixture of frustration and determination. "It is imperative that we heed these warnings and take concerted action to restore harmony with nature, safeguarding both our own well-being and the future of generations to come."

As he spoke, there was a palpable sense of urgency, a plea for action before it was too late. "We are witnessing the emergence of a generation driven by materialism, consumed by the pursuit of power, and disconnected from the intricate web of life that sustains us," he lamented. "This trajectory, if unchecked, poses a grave threat to the delicate balance of our ecosystems, hastening their decline at an alarming rate. Are we not treading a perilous path that imperils the future of generations to come?"

After a long pause, Shree Shambav's voice softened, filled with a sense of hope. "Akanksh," he said gently, "it is imperative that we heed this wake-up call and take proactive measures to safeguard our environment and preserve our ecosystems. Encouraging our children to reconnect with nature through simple yet meaningful actions, such as planting trees and nurturing them, can instil in them a sense of responsibility and stewardship towards the planet."

Unveiling the Depths of Parental Love

"For parents, love is not a mere sentiment, but a sacred vow to stand by us through every joy and sorrow, a commitment that knows no conditions or boundaries."

– Shree Shambav

In the quietude of dawn's embrace, as the sun cast its first golden rays upon the ancient city of Kanchipuram, Shree Shambav's voice echoed like a hymn of reverence. "Parents," he spoke, his words carrying the weight of centuries of wisdom, "are the silent architects of our lives. Their love, a fortress, unwavering and enduring, guides us through the labyrinth of existence. They are the threads that bind us, the anchors that steady us amidst life's tumultuous seas."

With each beat of the heart, parents offer the sacred gift of their unwavering devotion, their sacrifices etched into the very fabric of our being. From the tender embrace of infancy to the guiding hand of adolescence, they nurture and shape us, imparting wisdom with each whispered word and tender touch.

Their love transcends the confines of time and space, boundless and eternal. In their eyes, we are reflections of their hopes and dreams, their aspirations woven into the very essence of our existence. With every milestone achieved, every triumph celebrated, their hearts swell with pride, a testament to the unyielding bond that unites us.

Amidst the serene setting of Shree Shambav's discourse, where the gentle rustle of leaves danced in harmony with the whispered teachings of wisdom, a devoted soul named Apeksha found herself grappling with a question that weighed heavily on her heart. With furrowed brows and eyes clouded with sorrow, she summoned the courage to voice her inquiry. "Guruji," she began, her voice trembling with emotion, "why is it that some children, even after receiving a good education and securing prosperous careers, still choose to ill-treat their parents?"

With a tenderness that mirrored the warmth of a loving embrace, Shree Shambav's compassionate gaze softened as he listened to Apeksha's heartfelt plea. With a gentle smile, he extended a silent invitation for her to sit beside him, beckoning her to share in the depths of his wisdom through the storytelling art.

"Once upon a time," he began, his voice a soothing melody that echoed through the hushed ambiance, "in a quaint village nestled amidst emerald hills and azure skies, there lived a young man named Siddharth. Blessed with intellect and ambition, Siddharth embarked on a journey of knowledge, traversing the halls of esteemed institutions, and emerging with laurels of success adorning his brow."

Yet, amidst the glow of accolades and the promise of a bright future, Siddharth found himself ensnared in the labyrinth of worldly pursuits. Blinded by the allure of material wealth and societal acclaim, he forged ahead on the path of ambition, his heart growing cold and distant with each step taken in pursuit of success.

As Siddharth's fortunes soared, so too did his arrogance and disregard for those who had nurtured him with unwavering love and sacrifice. His parents, once revered as the pillars of his existence, now stood in the shadow of his towering ego, their pleas for affection drowned out by the cacophony of his ambitions.

With each passing day, Siddharth's parents bore the brunt of his callous indifference, their hearts heavy with the weight of unspoken anguish. Yet, they remained steadfast in their devotion, silently praying for the return of the son they had once known, the son who had been lost to the seductive allure of worldly acclaim.

As Siddharth's life unfolded with remarkable success, the glittering facade of material wealth and societal acclaim obscured his vision, shielding him from the profound depths of familial love. But fate, in its unfathomable wisdom, intervened, casting a shadow upon his once-bright horizon. The sudden loss of a dear friend, a mentor who had been his guiding light in business and personal growth, plunged Siddharth into the depths of despair, his soul torn asunder by the cruel hand of tragedy.

In the wake of profound loss, Siddharth found himself standing at the precipice of existence, grappling with the harsh reality of his own mortality. Amidst the deafening silence of his grief-stricken heart, he was forced to confront the bitter truth that his relentless pursuit of success had left him hollow, devoid of the one thing that truly mattered - love.

With a heart heavy with remorse and eyes blurred by tears, Siddharth embarked on a journey of redemption, guided by the faint whisper of his conscience and the flickering flame of hope.

After much hesitation and inner turmoil, Siddharth finally returned to the humble abode of his parents. With trepidation mingled with longing, he stood before them, his soul laid bare before the ones who had nurtured him with boundless love.

As Siddharth's mother enveloped him in a tender embrace, his tears mingled with hers as he uttered the words that weighed heavily on his heart. "I am sorry," he murmured, his voice choked with emotion. "I was blind to true love, chasing after fleeting pleasures instead of embracing the enduring happiness that was always within reach."

In the comforting embrace of his mother's unconditional love, Siddharth found solace amidst the turmoil that threatened to engulf him. The warmth of her embrace, a beacon of light in the darkness that had shrouded his heart for so long, offered a glimmer of hope amidst the despair.

Turning to his father, Siddharth was met with tear-filled eyes and a silent understanding that transcended words. With a heavy heart, he embraced his father, the weight of his remorse heavy upon his shoulders as he whispered, "I am sorry, I am truly sorry."

And in that moment, amidst the embrace of familial bonds that had weathered the trials of time, Siddharth found not only forgiveness but also the true essence of prosperity. For in the simple yet profound moments shared with his parents, he discovered the richness of a life lived with love and compassion, a treasure far greater than any material wealth could ever bestow.

As Shree Shambav's tale unfolded, Apeksha found herself swept away by a tide of emotions, tears glistening in her eyes as she was reminded of the fragile intricacies of human relationships and the enduring strength of love and forgiveness.

Shree Shambav's voice resonated with wisdom as he continued, his words piercing through the silence of the room. "Apeksha," he said softly, "it is amidst the darkest of times, in moments of despair and uncertainty, that the depth of a parent's love truly shines. With arms outstretched, they become beacons of light in the storm, offering solace amidst the encroaching shadows. In their embrace, we find refuge, strength, and the courage to navigate the trials that lie ahead."

And yet, Shree Shambav continued, his voice gentle but firm, "it is in the quiet moments, devoid of grand gestures or accolades, that the true essence of parental love is revealed. In the simple act of listening, of offering a comforting smile or a reassuring hug, they impart a sense of belonging, a feeling of being cherished and understood."

"For parents," Shree Shambav continued, his words weighted with reverence, "love is not merely a sentiment, but a sacred vow. It is a commitment to stand by our side through every joy and sorrow, every triumph and defeat. It is a love that knows no conditions, no boundaries, no end."

With a newfound understanding blooming within her, Apeksha vowed to cherish and honour her own parents with a reverence born of deep appreciation. In that moment, she recognised the truest treasure of all - the unwavering love of her parents, a priceless gift that surpassed all material wealth.

Embracing Wisdom

"Amidst the journey of self-discovery, every stumble becomes a stepping stone, guiding us towards the light of enlightenment."

– Shree Shambav

In the tranquil embrace of the village, where the hills whispered secrets to the sky and the forests sang melodies of ancient wisdom, Kai tended to his flock with a tender heart and a steady hand. Lumi, his faithful companion, trotted alongside him, their bond forged through years of shared solitude and silent understanding.

One brisk autumn morning, as the sun painted the horizon with strokes of gold and amber, Kai led his sheep to graze upon the dew-kissed grass. With each step, his mind danced with thoughts that lingered on the edge of understanding, pondering the mysteries that lay hidden within the vast expanse of the universe.

Lost in the labyrinth of his thoughts, Kai stumbled upon a secluded glade where an ancient cherry tree stood sentinel amidst a carpet of crimson leaves. Its branches reached skyward, as if reaching out to touch the heavens, and Kai felt drawn to its silent majesty, as if called by a force beyond his comprehension.

Beneath the shade of the cherry tree, Kai found solace in the embrace of nature, his soul stirred by the symphony of rustling leaves and the gentle caress of the breeze. As he closed his eyes and surrendered to the rhythm of the earth, he felt a profound sense of peace wash over him, like a warm blanket on a cold winter's night.

Upon awakening from his slumber, Kai's path intersected with a group of weary travellers, their faces etched with the lines of hardship and toil. Moved by compassion, Kai extended his hospitality, offering them shelter beneath his humble roof for the night.

As they journeyed to Kai's small hut, the sky above darkened, the wind whispered secrets of distant lands, and the stars cast their twinkling light upon the earth below. With weariness tugging at their limbs, the travellers welcomed the warmth of Kai's hearth and the comfort of his hospitality, finding a respite from the trials of their journey in the embrace of his humble abode.

In the quiet stillness of the night, as the world slumbered beneath a blanket of stars, Kai's heart overflowed with gratitude for the opportunity to offer kindness to strangers in need. And as sleep claimed him, he found solace in the knowledge that even in the darkest of nights, the light of compassion could illuminate the path toward a brighter tomorrow.

In the embrace of the dawn, where the golden hues of morning danced upon the canvas of the sky, Kai found himself amidst the tranquil beauty of his village. The air was alive with the symphony of nature, as birds greeted the day with joyful melodies, and the fragrance of blossoming flowers perfumed the breeze.

As the morning sun cast its warm embrace upon the earth, Shree Shambav gathered his disciples beneath the shade of a towering oak, their hearts open and eager to receive the wisdom that flowed from his lips like a gentle stream.

With a serene smile, Shree Shambav began to weave his tale, his words laden with the weight of ancient truths and timeless wisdom. "My dear disciples," he began, his voice a soothing balm to the soul, "let me share with you a story, a tale of transformation and the power of self-discovery."

He paused, allowing the words to linger in the air like the soft caress of a gentle breeze, before continuing.

As the story unfolded, Padma, one of the devoted disciples, turned to Kai with a gentle smile. "Join us, Kai," she urged, her eyes alight with the promise of enlightenment.

Kai's voice, though soft, carried the weight of a lifetime of introspection. "I am born into humble beginnings. I knew only the simplicity of rural life, my days spent tending to his flock with unwavering dedication and boundless love. I have born worthless; I live worthless and I will die worthless."

He continued, "I am a good shepherd, and I can only be a good shepherd. Anything more I expect would be out of greed."

Padma nodded, her expression understanding. "For in the presence of our master, even the most humble of souls can find wisdom beyond measure."

With a hesitant nod, Kai stepped forward, his heart heavy with the weight of his own perceived insignificance. "I am but a simple shepherd," he confessed, his voice tinged with self-doubt. "Born into poverty, with nothing to my name but a small hut and a few sheep. What wisdom could I possibly gather, and how could it possibly help me?"

Padma's smile only widened; her faith unwavering in the face of Kai's uncertainty. "You underestimate the power of your own journey, Kai," she replied, her words gentle yet firm. "For it is often in the most unlikely of places that we find the greatest treasures."

With Padma's encouragement, Kai allowed himself to be drawn into the embrace of the discourse, his heart open to the possibility of newfound understanding and enlightenment. And as he listened to the timeless wisdom that flowed from Shree Shambav's lips, he felt a stirring within his soul - a glimmer of hope that perhaps, in the tapestry of his own life, there lay hidden depths of meaning and purpose yet to be discovered.

With a serene smile, Shree Shambav began, his eyes twinkling with wisdom. "Let me share with you a tale of transformation, of the journey from imperfection to greatness."

He paused, allowing his words to sink in, before continuing, "Consider the journey of milk. When it sours, it becomes yoghurt, a substance more valuable than its previous form. And if it further ages, it transforms into cheese, surpassing both milk and yoghurt in worth. Similarly, grape juice, when it turns sour, becomes wine, a prized elixir sought after by many."

The disciples listened intently; their minds captivated by the metaphorical tale woven by their beloved master. Shree Shambav smiled, seeing their rapt attention, before he continued.

Shree Shambav said, "Diamonds, those exquisite gems that capture the imagination with their brilliance and allure, are formed deep within the Earth's mantle over millions to billions of years. The process begins with carbon atoms being subjected to extreme pressure and temperature conditions, typically found at depths of 87 to 118 miles beneath the Earth's surface."

Under these intense conditions, carbon atoms bond together in a unique arrangement, forming the crystalline structure of a diamond. As the carbon-rich material moves closer to the Earth's surface through volcanic activity, it cools and solidifies, trapping the diamond crystals within.

This journey from deep within the Earth to the surface can take millions of years, during which time the diamonds are subjected to further geological processes and upheavals. Eventually, some diamonds are brought closer to the surface through volcanic eruptions, where they can be discovered and mined.

After a raw diamond is mined from the Earth, it undergoes a series of meticulous processes to transform it into the stunning gemstones we admire. First, the raw diamond is cut. Following cutting, the diamond undergoes polishing, a meticulous process that involves grinding away any imperfections and refining the facets to enhance its shine and lustre. The result is a breathtakingly beautiful diamond, with dazzling brilliance and unmatched elegance.

The beauty of a diamond lies not only in its physical structure but also in the remarkable journey it takes to come into existence. Each diamond is a testament to the incredible forces of nature and the passage of time, making it a symbol of endurance, strength, and timeless beauty.

"You see, my dear disciples, life mirrors this process of transformation. We all encounter setbacks and failures, but it is not these moments that define us. Rather, it is how we learn and grow from them."

Expounding on his point, Shree Shambav continued, "It matters not where or how we are born. What truly matters is how we choose to live our lives."

He paused, allowing his words to resonate with the disciples, before continuing, "Every soul has a purpose on this earth. No soul is born worthless, and no soul dies worthless. Each moment of life is an opportunity to celebrate and grow. Every obstacle we face is a chance to elevate ourselves."

Kai opened his eyes, his heart brimming with newfound understanding. He realised that life, much like milk and grape juice, was a journey of transformation - a journey filled with twists and turns, ups and downs.

Shree Shambav continued, his voice resonating with the weight of ancient truths, "In the divine creation, every soul has a purpose on this earth, akin to the path of a river carving through the earth, encountering rocks and bends, but always moving towards the vast ocean of existence. The hurdles we face, the trials we endure, they are the chisel strokes of the divine sculptor, shaping us into vessels of wisdom and compassion."

With renewed purpose, Kai felt as though he stood at the threshold of a new dawn, his spirit ignited by the flame of wisdom that emanated from Shree Shambav's teachings. He realised that his journey was just beginning - that each stumble, each misstep, held within it the seeds of transformation, waiting to bloom beneath the nurturing light of self-discovery.

And so, guided by the timeless wisdom of Shree Shambav, Kai embraced the challenges that lay ahead, his heart brimming with the knowledge that true enlightenment lay not in the absence of mistakes, but in the courage to confront them head-on - to see in them the raw material of growth and self-realisation.

As he turned to Padma, gratitude flooded Kai's soul like a gentle stream, washing away the remnants of doubt and uncertainty. "Thank you," he whispered, his voice tinged with emotion. "For in your guidance, I have found the courage to embark on this transformative journey."

With a newfound sense of purpose and clarity, Kai felt as though he had shed the weight of the world from his shoulders. He walked with lightness in his step, his heart buoyed by the promise of self-discovery and growth that lay ahead.

Eternal Bonds

"Even in the face of neglect, a parent's love remains steadfast, a beacon of unconditional grace and endless compassion. They see their own worth reflected in our achievements, tirelessly wishing for our well-being and success."

\- *Shree Shambav*

One day, while travelling through the sacred city of Kanchipuram, Shree Shambav and his devotees found themselves surrounded by the silent whispers of the wind, the aroma of sandalwood, and the vibrant colours of turmeric and Kumkum. The air was thick with divinity. As they walked, they noticed an old lady sitting on the temple steps. Her name was Kamala, and her face was etched with sadness and anxiety, waiting for someone who never came.

Avinash, moved by her sorrowful presence, approached a man named Karna, who was sitting beside her. "Why does this old lady seem so distressed?" Avinash asked softly.

Karna sighed deeply and began to explain, "Kamala was once a wealthy landlord, dedicating her life to her only son. She invested everything in him—her time, love, and wealth. The boy grew up to be an engineer and settled in a distant place. Despite his persistent pleas for her to join him, she always refused, stating she had to manage their estate in India."

Karna's voice grew softer, laden with sorrow. "One day, her son came to visit her unexpectedly. He begged her to sell all her property and move with him. Reluctantly, under his insistent pressure, Kamala agreed. She sold everything and handed the money over to her son. On the day they were supposed to leave, he asked her to wait at the railway station with her bags while he fetched some refreshments for their journey."

Karna paused, his eyes reflecting the weight of Kamala's suffering. "Hours turned into days, but her son never returned. He vanished with all her precious belongings and money. Kamala searched for him everywhere, but he was gone. Now, she survives on the charity of temple-goers and by doing small jobs around the temple. The mother who sacrificed everything for her son is now reduced to a life of hardship and loneliness in her old age. Who is to blame? The son for his treachery, or the mother for her blind faith in him?"

Padma and Avinash's eyes welled up with tears, the weight of Kamala's story hanging heavily in the air. Karna continued, "Kamala still clings to the hope that her son will return one day, believing he must be searching for her."

As they continued their journey, a long silence enveloped the group. They eventually settled outside the temple beneath a large banyan tree. After a moment of quiet reflection, Avinash turned to Shree Shambav and asked, "Why should one take care of their old parents? Why don't parents plan for their later years? Do they really need children?"

Shree Shambav, with a gentle yet profound expression, replied, "Avinash, when you speak about your parents, particularly your mother, you must be very precise and careful. You should handle them with utmost care and great precision, for they are precious. Look at what we have done to them. We feel they are a burden, that they are useless, that they have less sense, that they don't understand."

Shree Shambav's voice took on a deeper tone. "Avinash, truth is unbearable. But it is a naked fact that hardly anyone cares for their parents in their old age, the last phase of human life. A child is brought up and taken care of until they gain their own sense of direction. Guidance, suggestions, and above all, food and nutrition, are provided by the parents to make their children physically and mentally strong. Parents know their duty and responsibility. They desperately endeavour to create a good future for their kids, often without considering the adverse effects of their love and affection in this material world."

He continued, "In modern society, when children grow up, earn money, and enjoy modern facilities, they often forget the sacrifices their parents made for them. They forget the pain their parents endured to pave the way for their success. If an old mother's spectacles break or an old father wants some delicious food, they are ignored or met with harsh words from their now-grown children."

Shree Shambav's eyes were filled with both sorrow and compassion as he spoke. "Modern children often see their parents as a financial burden, especially when it comes to medical expenses. Even those who are well-educated and sensible can behave abnormally towards their old parents. They fail to understand their parents' feelings and emotions, treating relationships as mere transactions based on a 'give and take' policy. To many, their parents have become nothing more than a burden."

After a long pause, Shree Shambav's voice softened. "Parents have lost their hopes in their lives, lost hope in their children. We make them feel like their efforts were in vain. Our responsibility is to give them confidence, importance, clarity, and the strength they once gavc us."

He added with heartfelt conviction, "Even if children turn away from their parents, those beautiful souls always keep their children in their hearts, always wish for their well-being and success. A parent sees their life's work reflected in their children's achievements, and their love is unwavering, regardless of the circumstances. Parents are the eternal well-wishers, the ones who bless you without conditions.

A child is the lifeblood of a family, and equally, the presence of parents is the bedrock of our existence. They are not merely old; they are a treasure trove of wisdom. Parents are not just weary; they are tireless in their devotion. Elders are not a burden; they bear our burdens with grace. Parents should not be seen as the last to be considered; they are the very foundation upon which we stand.

A house without elders is like a tree stripped of its leaves, a butterfly devoid of its vibrant colours, a peacock without its mesmerising dance. Their presence adds depth, colour, and beauty to our lives, making our journey rich and fulfilling."

Shree Shambav with a poignant reflection, "From our birth to death, from the mother's womb to the graveyard, from the cradle to the mortuary box, our lives are shaped by the sacrifices of our elders. They deserve our utmost respect and care, for they are the roots that sustain the tree of our lives."

Shree Shambav, after a moment of reflection, said, "Even in the face of neglect, a parent's love remains unwavering—a beacon of unconditional grace and boundless compassion. They see their own worth mirrored in our achievements, endlessly wishing for our well-being and success."

Embracing Change

"In moments of deep humility and awe, we find the strength to forgive, to understand, and ultimately, to transform our lives and the lives of others for the better."

- *Shree Shambav*

Shree Shambav during his discourse said, "A few years ago, the river used to flow along this path." His eyes seemed to gaze into the past, recalling the vibrant scene vividly. "We could see greenery all around, with abundant plants, colourful flowers, fluttering butterflies, humming bees, singing birds, and fish happily swimming in the water. There were storks carefully watching for their prey and hissing snakes. This place was full of life, and vibrant. And now, see this place as deserted."

Inquisitive devotee Akanksh asked, "Why did this river dry up?"

Shree Shambav's expression softened with empathy. "There are many reasons. Deforestation has led to scanty rainfall, but a major reason is the construction of a dam. The flow of the river has been blocked by the dam. Now, hardly any water overflows from the dam, and the path it once traversed slowly died. All living organisms that depended on it also perished."

Akanksh pondered aloud, "So, building the dam was wrong?"

Shree Shambav shook his head gently. "No, but ignoring the equilibrium of the system or nature is wrong."

Apeksha, intrigued by the discussion, asked, "In what ways can embracing personal change impact your relationships with others and the broader community?"

Shree Shambav nodded thoughtfully. "Let me narrate a story." His tone became measured, drawing the listeners into the tale. "Salim lived in a city dealing with scraps. Through sheer hard work, he began to earn money and diversified his business, eventually becoming wealthy. As money poured in, so did ego. He lost touch with reality, convinced of his sharp intelligence and success. This led him to disrespect his fellowmen and supporters."

"Upon hearing of a lucrative opportunity in a nearby city, Salim planned his journey, which was a hundred miles away. He hired a sophisticated cart pulled by a horse."

Salim leaned back in the cart, the early morning sun casting a golden hue over the journey ahead. Turning to the cart driver, he asked with a hint of impatience, "What's your name?"

The cart driver, Fakir, replied in a calm, measured tone, "My name is Fakir, and my fare is five silver coins."

"Fine," Salim nodded, "but I may need to overstay in the nearby city if things don't go as planned."

Fakir considered for a moment before responding, "I am fine with that, but I will need an advance payment. It's for my wife's daily expenses."

Salim chuckled dismissively, "How can I pay you before even getting into the cart?"

Fakir smiled patiently, "My house is only half an hour from your place of business in the city. You can pay me when we arrive."

Agreeing reluctantly, Salim settled into the cart, and they set off early morning. As they travelled, Salim's demeanour grew increasingly disrespectful towards Fakir, boasting about his rise from humble beginnings to prosperity. Along the jungle route, they spotted an old man asleep under a massive tree. As they approached, the cart suddenly stopped, refusing to move forward.

Fakir tried to coax the horse onward, but it remained stubbornly still. Concerned, he got down and approached the old man, only to find someone he dreaded seeing in such a vulnerable state.

Meanwhile, Salim's voice cut through the air impatiently, "You fool! Why are you wasting my time? You clearly don't understand the value of time—that's why you're poor. For me, every minute counts."

Fakir, torn between duty and compassion, glanced back at Salim with tears welling in his eyes. Feeling helpless, he reluctantly left the old man and resumed the journey.

Finally arriving at their destination, Fakir turned to Salim and calmly requested the advance payment they had agreed upon. Without a word, Salim handed over the coins, and Fakir nodded. "I'll return in two hours," he said quietly before disappearing into the bustling city streets.

Fakir stood at his door, a heavy heart weighing him down as he knocked. The door creaked open, revealing his wife, tears glistening in her eyes. She looked at him with a mix of sorrow and concern, her voice trembling as she spoke, "Do you know what happened today?"

Curious yet apprehensive, Fakir asked softly, "What happened?"

His wife took a deep breath, her voice quivering with emotion. "Our landlord visited us today. He stood before his statue with tears streaming down his face, and then he left."

Fakir nodded solemnly, his heart sinking at the news. "Yes, dear, I saw him on my way back. It pained me to see his despair."

His wife looked at him with a hopeful glimmer in her eyes. "Did you speak to him?"

Fakir's expression turned sorrowful. "No," he admitted regretfully, "I didn't have the privilege of spending time with him."

Tears welled up in Fakir's eyes as he continued, "Let me do something about it. We should bring him to the city and offer our help."

His wife nodded in agreement, her voice firm with resolve. "Yes, we must." She rallied their neighbours together, and together they devised a plan to bring the landlord, Sitaraman, back to the town and provide him with the support he needed.

The townspeople gathered around Sitaraman under the tree where they had found him, leaning heavily against its trunk. Tears flowed freely as they expressed their deep concern and love for him, their voices trembling with emotion. They reassured him, "We are here for you. We are like seeds that have grown into trees to shelter you. Please don't think you are alone."

Their words hung heavy in the air, a testament to the compassion and unity of the community. They were determined to lift Sitaraman out of his misery and show him that he was cherished and supported, no matter the circumstances.

Sitaraman's words echoed softly amidst the circle of concerned faces. "Please, do not be upset," he began, his voice warm but tinged with a deep sorrow. "I appreciate your kindness, but I am fine."

He paused, gathering his thoughts before continuing with a heavy heart, "I have experienced sadness, disappointment, and even cursed the divine for my plight. I lost my beloved wife in a tragic accident, my children succumbed to illness, and calamities swept away my wealth. I became a wanderer, adrift for over five years. In my final moments of despair, I ventured to your city to find my grandmother's place, only to discover it lost to time. Yet, to my astonishment, I stumbled upon my own statue, surrounded by people in tears. In that moment, the burdens that weighed me down felt as light as feathers. All my pain melted away into a profound sense of happiness."

He looked around at the attentive faces, his eyes shimmering with gratitude. "The respect and kindness you have shown me, the reverence you have bestowed upon me... How could I possibly bring more pain to you by revealing my helplessness?"

After a moment of reflection, Sitaraman's expression softened. "I feel relieved, perhaps the happiest I have ever been. The divine has been exceedingly kind to me."

Moved by the heartfelt plea of the townspeople, Sitaraman finally relented. "Because of your unwavering care and compassion, I will return," he announced quietly. "If you continue to support me in this way, I will have no reason to continue suffering."

As they journeyed back to the town, one of the townspeople spoke up, his voice filled with sincerity. "Sir, all your properties and your house remain intact. They have been cared for diligently by our community. While the maintenance may not be perfect, they are ready for you to occupy whenever you choose."

Sitaraman's heart swelled with gratitude at the news, overwhelmed by the generosity and loyalty of the surrounding people. It was a humbling reminder of the power of community and the enduring bonds of compassion that transcended time and circumstance.

The person who had been caring for Sitaraman's house fell to his feet, tears streaming down his face as he cried aloud, "Why did you leave us?" He eagerly showed Sitaraman around the house, pointing out photographs that adorned the walls. Among them were pictures of Sitaraman's father and mother, capturing moments from a past that now seemed distant yet vivid in memory.

As Sitaraman gazed at these images, a flood of emotions engulfed him. He recalled his childhood days spent in this very house, the laughter echoing through the rooms, and the warmth of his parents' love that had shaped his early years. Destiny had pulled him away from this place, and now, it seemed, that same destiny had guided him back.

Amidst these memories, Sitaraman remembered something his father had once mentioned—an important note kept in a box, hidden in the locker room adjacent to the bedroom. With trembling hands and a heart heavy with anticipation, Sitaraman finally unlocked the door and retrieved the box. Inside, he found a letter from his father, written with a mixture of regret and hope.

"One can face any difficulty in life," the note began, "but there is a truth I have kept hidden from you. After years of unsuccessful attempts to conceive, your mother and I sought the help of a Siddha medicine practitioner. We spent many days in his ashram undergoing treatments, and during that time, I fell in love with a woman named Shobha. Due to societal pressures, she bore a son for me, a truth I have concealed from everyone, including you."

Sitaraman's heart sank as he absorbed these words, grappling with the weight of the revelation. His father continued, "In this box, I have enclosed a photograph of Shobha and her son, your half-brother. This secret has haunted me for years, burdened by the deception I have carried. I lacked the courage to reveal the truth to your mother or to you. I ask you now to accept him as your brother, and together, honour our family's legacy and continue to serve the people of this town."

Overwhelmed by conflicting emotions of betrayal and compassion, Sitaraman traced the lines of his father's confession, feeling the weight of generations of secrets and decisions that had shaped their family's history. Yet, amidst the turmoil, there was also a profound sense of understanding and forgiveness—an acknowledgment of the complexities of human relationships and the enduring bonds of love that transcended the trials of life.

As he closed the box and locked away the truth that had been revealed, Sitaraman knew that the path forward would be challenging, but he also felt a newfound resolve to embrace his father's legacy of compassion and integrity. With a deep breath, he turned to the caretaker and said softly, "Thank you for taking care of our home. Now, let us work together to honour the past and build a future that upholds the values my father held dear."

With trembling hands, Sitaraman slowly opened the cover to see the pictures. To his shock, the man who had been looking after his wealth and palace was his brother, Advaitha. Tears welled up in his eyes as the realisation dawned on him. Overcome with emotion, he rushed to Advaitha and embraced him tightly, saying, "I thought I had lost everything, but now I realise I have everything I need right here. I was lost in my own world, blind to the surrounding blessings."

Advaitha, equally moved, returned the embrace with tears of his own. "Brother, we are family, bound by blood and love. No matter the distance or the secrets, we are here for each other."

Turning to Fakir and the gathered townspeople, Sitaraman's voice broke with gratitude, "I am grateful to you all, and to the people of this town, for your kindness and for helping me to rebuild what I thought was lost. Your support and compassion have shown me the true wealth of life—family, community, and love."

Fakir stepped forward, his eyes glistening with tears. "Sir, it is we who are honoured to have you back among us. Your father's legacy lives on through you, and together, we will continue to uphold the values of generosity and compassion that he instilled in this town."

The townspeople gathered around, their faces reflecting a shared sense of joy and relief. They knew that their community was stronger with Sitaraman's return, and they pledged to support him in reclaiming his rightful place.

As the sun set, casting a golden glow over the town, Sitaraman stood with his brother, Fakir, and the townspeople, feeling a profound sense of belonging and purpose. He understood now that his journey had come full circle, bringing him back to the roots of his heritage, where love and unity would guide them all into a brighter future.

Fakir and the others, their hearts heavy with emotion, slowly dispersed from the poignant scene. Fakir returned to Salim to continue their journey, his thoughts still lingering on Sitaraman's story. Meanwhile, Salim had overheard the tale from another merchant but remained unmoved. With a dismissive wave, he said, "He was senseless about his wealth. God gave him everything, but he threw it all away. Why do people talk so highly of him?"

As they resumed their journey, Salim's curiosity got the better of him. "Fakir, who is this, Sitaraman? Why do people talk great about him? To me, he's just a fool who wasted his fortune."

Fakir's patience was wearing thin. He replied with a strained calmness, "We should not speak ill of someone we do not understand. Sitaraman may be a godlike figure to many. We should respect that."

Salim, irritated, snapped, "And you think you can teach me how to behave?"

At this, Fakir lost his composure. With a sharp, decisive motion, he stopped the cart. "Get down from my carriage," he demanded, his voice trembling with suppressed anger. The evening was descending, and the surrounding forest was alive with the sounds of settling birds and croaking frogs, the air cool and fresh from recent rain.

Salim stood there, stunned, and bewildered. As the reality of spending a night alone in the dense forest dawned on him, fear crept in. He ran after Fakir, calling out, "I'm sorry! I shouldn't have started this conversation. I didn't mean to offend you."

Fakir paused, tears glistening in his eyes. Salim, genuinely concerned, asked, "Why are you so upset?"

Fakir took a deep breath, his voice soft but filled with emotion. "Salim, you see only wealth and success in material terms. Sitaraman's story isn't about loss; it's about the strength to endure unimaginable pain and still find compassion. He lost everything dear to him but gained the love and respect of an entire community through his humility and kindness. When you dismiss his life as folly, you disregard the profound human experiences that define true worth."

Salim listened, the weight of Fakir's words sinking in. He realised that his narrow perspective had blinded him to the deeper values that Sitaraman embodied—values that Fakir and the townspeople cherished. The journey back was silent, each man lost in his own thoughts, the forest around them whispering secrets of resilience and redemption.

Fakir, after a long, reflective silence, finally spoke, his voice tinged with both reverence and sorrow. "Sir, do you know whose cart you are travelling in? This is my landlord's carriage. I used to drive for him. My family has benefited immensely from his kindness. To us and the twelve surrounding villages, he is like a god."

He paused, gathering his thoughts, then continued with a heavy heart. "Do you know why the horse stopped in the middle of the jungle? It is because that horse belongs to my landlord. Even the horse has gratitude for what Sitaraman has done. Yet, you forced me to ignore him and keep driving when we came to the city."

Fakir's eyes welled up with tears, and his voice broke. "You see him as poor, but in our eyes, he is the wealthiest person. His wealth is not in material possessions but in the hearts, he has touched and the lives he has saved."

Hearing the depth of Fakir's devotion and the gravity of his words, tears started to flow from Salim's eyes, unbidden. He felt a profound sense of shame for his actions and begged for forgiveness. "I'm sorry, Fakir. I didn't understand. I want to meet this great person."

As they journeyed back, Fakir shared stories of Sitaraman and his family, his voice a mixture of pride and pain. "Every drop of blood in my body, and my family's, is indebted to the Sitaraman family. They have been our protectors, our benefactors."

Salim listened intently, his heart heavy with the realisation of his ignorance. He began to see the true measure of a person was not in their material wealth but in the love and respect they garnered from others.

When they finally reached the town, Fakir took Salim to meet Sitaraman. The old man was seated in his chair, his face etched with lines of both wisdom and sorrow, yet emanating a profound serenity. Despite the hardships he had endured, there was a timeless grace about him that commanded respect. Salim approached with a heart heavy with remorse and a newfound humility. Bowing deeply, he said, "Sir, I have heard much about you and your family. I am deeply sorry for my earlier disrespect. I wish to learn from you."

Salim's voice trembled with genuine reverence as he continued, "I cannot believe my eyes. Can someone truly be an example, an inspiration, a godly figure for so many people? In my eyes, you are divine. We all search for the divine, but divinity lies within ourselves. You have helped me understand what I am, what I have achieved, and what I am pursuing. This journey has given me a new dimension in my life."

Sitaraman looked at Salim, his eyes filled with a gentle understanding that seemed to see straight into Salim's soul. "We all make mistakes, my son. What matters is that we learn from them and strive to be better."

Salim felt a profound sense of peace wash over him, a weight lifting from his shoulders. He knew his life had been irrevocably changed by this encounter. What had begun as a pursuit of wealth had ended with the discovery of a richer, more meaningful existence.

Turning to Fakir, Salim said with heartfelt gratitude, "I am thankful to you, Fakir, for revealing the truth that was hidden from me. You have guided me on a journey of life, breaking the shell to show me a better vision of 'who I am.'"

Fakir, tears glistening in his eyes, nodded. "It was my duty, Salim. The Sitaraman family has been a pillar for us all, teaching us the true meaning of life and community."

Sitaraman, with a gentle smile, added, "I have realised from my people 'who I am.' Their respect and love have shown me my true worth."

Salim, overwhelmed by the depth of the moment, felt tears welling up in his eyes again, but this time they were tears of joy and enlightenment. He knelt before Sitaraman and said, "I pledge to honour your legacy by living a life of compassion and humility. I understand now that true wealth lies not in material possessions but in the hearts, we touch and the lives we uplift."

Sitaraman placed a hand on Salim's shoulder, his touch light but filled with profound warmth. "Rise, Salim. Let your journey of self-discovery inspire others. Be the light that guides them, just as you have found your own path."

As Salim stood up, he felt a profound sense of purpose and connection. The man who had begun his journey driven by ambition now understood that true fulfilment came from understanding and embracing the divine within oneself and others. The town's people, witnessing this transformation, felt a renewed sense of unity and hope, knowing that the legacy of compassion and integrity would continue through Salim's newfound wisdom.

As Salim stood up, he felt a deep sense of purpose and connection. The man who had begun his journey driven by ambition now understood that true fulfilment came from understanding and embracing the divine within oneself and others. The townspeople, witnessing this transformation, felt a renewed sense of unity and hope, knowing that the legacy of compassion and integrity would continue through Salim's newfound wisdom.

A Father's Love

"Love is not always spoken—it is stitched into the fabric of life, woven through silent gestures, unwavering patience, and the warmth that shields us when we are too young to understand."

- *Shree Shambav*

Shambav and his devoted disciples walked through the dusty paths of a quiet village. The golden hue of the setting sun bathed the land in an ethereal glow, but amidst the evening's tranquility, an unsettling scene unfolded before their eyes. A young man, Ganesan, stood in heated argument with his father, Ramesh, his words sharp as arrows, cutting deep into the heart of the old man.

Tears welled in Ramesh's eyes as one of the devotees, moved by compassion, stepped forward and asked, "Why are you so sad, O wise one?"

The old man, his voice trembling with grief, replied, "My father gave me two acres of land. I toiled day and night, battling droughts and storms, plowing the earth with my bare hands. With sweat and sacrifice, I expanded it to ten acres. I built a home—not just of bricks and mortar, but of love and warmth. I educated my son, ensured he lacked nothing, and watched with pride as he rose to work in a grand city firm. Yet today, he stands before me, questioning my worth as a father, asking—'What have you done for me?'"

A profound silence followed. Shambav, who had been observing the scene, said nothing. Without a word, he turned away and left the village.

Two days passed. Then, as if bound by an unseen thread, Shambav led his disciples back to the same village. They found Ramesh standing at his doorstep, sorrow weighing down his frame like an ancient tree withering under the burden of its own branches. His son, Ganesan, stood beside him, his face hardened with determination. The argument had escalated—he was now demanding that his father sell their land and home, insisting that the money would be better invested in city properties.

Shambav watched in silence, his deep eyes unreadable. Then, after what seemed an eternity, he called for Ganesan. The young man hesitated. He had no desire to speak with a wandering sage, but at the repeated urging of the devotees, he reluctantly approached.

Shambav gazed at him for a long time before speaking. His voice was neither harsh nor pleading, but held a quiet, compelling strength. "Ganesan, let me share a story with you."

"Once, in the vast expanse of time, an old monk walked the land, his soul unburdened by possessions, yet rich with wisdom. One winter, he met a young boy, shivering under the unforgiving sky, his lips blue, his tiny hands trembling. Moved by compassion, the monk took off his only woolen shawl and wrapped it around the child, offering warmth against the merciless cold."

"Months passed. By fate or by divine design, their paths crossed again. The young boy, now named Mateo, greeted the monk, still draped in the same shawl. The monk, curious, asked, 'Mateo, what became of the shawl I gave you?'"

"Mateo smiled and replied, 'Master, I turned it into a blanket to guard me against the night's chill.'"

"The monk nodded, intrigued. 'And the blanket before that?'"

"Mateo, eyes shining with warmth, said, 'It became a bed cover, a resting place for my weary body.'"

"The monk, with a gentle laugh, continued, 'And before that?'"

"Mateo beamed, 'It became a pillow cover, a soft cradle for my dreams.'"

"The monk, delighted by the boy's wisdom, pressed further, 'And the pillow cover?'"

"Mateo, now radiating joy, said, 'It became a mat, the very ground I kneel upon.'"

"The monk's eyes twinkled. 'And the mat before that?'"

"With a quiet reverence, Mateo whispered, 'I unraveled the threads and turned them into wicks for my lamp, so that even in darkness, I could have light.'"

"The monk smiled, not just at Mateo's ingenuity, but at the profound truth within it. He placed a silent blessing upon the boy and walked away, knowing that the shawl had never faded—it had only transformed, finding new purpose at every stage, serving in ways that were unseen yet invaluable."

Shambav paused, his eyes locking onto Ganesan's. The air between them felt heavy, charged with meaning.

"Tell me, Ganesan," he asked, his voice soft yet piercing, "Was the shawl ever wasted?"

Ganesan stood silent. Something in his heart shifted, like the first crack in an ice-covered lake.

"Your father," Shambav continued, "is that shawl. He was once a son, like you. He inherited little, but instead of spending it, he multiplied it. He shielded you from the storms of life. When you were young, he was the blanket that kept you warm. When you needed guidance, he was the bed that gave you rest. When you pursued your dreams, he became the lamp, burning away silently so that you could have light. And now, in his twilight years, you stand here, questioning his worth, demanding his sacrifice, forgetting that all you stand upon today was woven from the threads of his love, toil, and patience."

Ganesan lowered his gaze. The world around him seemed unchanged, yet something within him had been shaken loose, something he had long ignored. His father had given him everything—not just land or a house, but years of unspoken sacrifices, a lifetime of love that had quietly transformed, repurposed, and served him in ways he had never noticed.

For the first time in a long while, he looked at his father—not as an old man, but as a being who had once been strong, hopeful, and giving. A man who had poured every ounce of himself into his son's future.

Silence lingered. Then, with a heavy breath, Ganesan turned toward his father. His lips parted, but no words came—only a welling of emotion, too vast to be spoken.

Shambav said no more. He had planted the seed; it was up to Ganesan to let it grow.

As the sun dipped below the horizon, casting the village in hues of amber and gold, the devotees watched in quiet reverence. The measure of a father's love, like the thread of a humble shawl, was not in what it was, but in how it had transformed, over and over, to serve and shelter without ever asking for anything in return.

And in that moment, Ganesan finally understood.

The Window of Perception

"Two souls may stand before the same horizon—one sees a sunset, the other a dawn. Perception shapes destiny."

- *Shree Shambav*

The golden hues of dawn painted the sky as Shambav and his devotees travelled through a quiet village nestled in the heart of India. Their journey was not just one of miles but of wisdom, seeking answers to the countless questions life presented.

As they walked through the bustling market, a devotee named Rajan, troubled by a recent incident, approached Master. "Master," he said, his voice heavy with contemplation, "why is it that some people see suffering and despair, while others see opportunity and growth? Why does one become rich and another poor, even when faced with the same reality?"

Guruji smiled gently, sensing the depth of Rajan's inquiry. He motioned for the group to gather under a large banyan tree, its roots entwined like the unseen threads of destiny. "Let me tell you a story," he said, his voice calm yet powerful, carrying the weight of countless truths.

The Two Travellers

Many years ago, two men, Rajesh and Varun, arrived from a distant land, both eager to explore its vast landscapes and immerse themselves in its culture. One morning, as they gazed out of the window of their train, a sight caught their attention—hundreds of barefoot children running through the dusty streets, their feet hardened by years of walking on scorching earth.

Rajesh felt his heart sink. His eyes welled up with tears as he whispered, "This is heartbreaking. These people have nothing… Look at them, walking without shoes! How cruel fate has been to them." He turned away, unable to bear the sight.

Varun, sitting beside him, observed the same scene but saw something different. His eyes gleamed with an idea. "Rajesh," he said, "do you see what I see? This is not just suffering—this is a need, an opportunity to make a difference! If these people had access to affordable shoes, their lives could change. What if we start a business making shoes for them?"

Rajesh scoffed. "Business? How can you think of money when you see suffering?"

But Varun was undeterred. With determination, he set up a small shoe factory, hiring local artisans and workers, ensuring that the poorest could afford quality footwear. His company grew beyond imagination, and soon, he became one of the most successful entrepreneurs in the country.

Years passed. One day, Rajesh, now struggling to make ends meet, found himself applying for a job. As fate would have it, he walked into Varun's company, seeking employment. He was greeted by the sight of thousands of workers, earning their livelihood by making shoes—shoes that reached every corner of the nation, ensuring no child had to walk barefoot.

Rajesh looked around in astonishment. "You saw the same thing I did… yet you turned it into something beautiful," he admitted, his voice tinged with regret.

Varun placed a hand on his shoulder. "The world is as we choose to see it, my friend. Some see despair, while others see the seeds of change."

As Master finished his story, the devotees sat in deep thought. Rajan, who had posed the question, bowed his head. "I understand now, Guruji. It is not what we see, but how we perceive it. Wisdom is not just in observing the world, but in transforming it."

Guruji smiled. "Exactly. Wealth is not only measured in money. A rich mind sees potential, while a poor mind sees limitations. Some become rich, and some become poor—not just in materialistic terms, but in wisdom, in vision, and in the ability to create change."

As the devotees continued their journey, Rajan walked with a lighter heart, his mind no longer clouded by doubt. He had found his answer—not in words alone, but in the realisation that perspective shapes destiny.

The Eyes That Never Cried

"A mother's love never leaves—it lingers in the air we breathe, in the lessons we carry, and in the silence where we finally understand."

- *Shree Shambav*

The morning sun painted the meadows in hues of gold as Shambav and his devotees wandered into a serene village. The journey had been long, the roads unkind, but the sight of lush green fields and the gentle murmur of flowing water offered a moment of solace.

At dawn, after a night of rest, the devotees ventured out for a stroll. The air was crisp, and birdsong filled the sky. Yet, amidst this peaceful setting, an unsettling scene caught their attention. A young man stood outside a humble hut, shouting at an elderly woman. His words were sharp, laced with disgust, and his face twisted in anger. The old woman, frail and bent with age, stood in silence, her wrinkled hands trembling as she clutched the edge of her tattered saree.

One of the devotees, Sam, unable to contain his anguish, stepped forward and asked, "Why do you speak to her in such a manner?"

The young man turned, his gaze cold and unfeeling. "She is my mother," he spat. "She is filthy, wretched, and an embarrassment. I feel ashamed to call her my own."

A heavy silence followed. The devotees looked at the woman, her eyes sunken yet holding a sorrow deeper than words could express. They turned back to the young man, hoping to reason with him, but he had already walked away, indifferent and unbothered.

With heavy hearts, Sam and the others returned to their resting place, their minds restless with grief. When Shambav saw the sadness on their faces, he asked, "Sam, why do you look troubled?"

Sam narrated the incident, expecting words of wisdom, expecting Shambav to intervene, to guide, to restore justice. But to his surprise, Shambav merely listened, then quietly said, "Let us have our morning meal," and continued their journey.

The devotees were perplexed. Had their master not understood the gravity of the situation? How could he remain silent in the face of such cruelty?

Days passed, yet the incident continued to weigh heavily on Sam's heart. Doubt crept into his mind—was silence the answer to suffering? Why had their revered master not done anything to help the old woman?

Then, fate wove its web in an unexpected way. In another village, as they settled for the evening, they saw the same young man, now alone, sitting outside a small inn. This time, it was Shambav who approached him.

Introducing himself with warmth, Shambav sat beside the young man, who seemed hesitant yet curious. After a brief exchange, Shambav said, "Let me tell you a story…"

"In a distant village, there lived a boy named Ajay. His mother had only one eye. He hated her for it.

She was poor, running a small tea shop to provide for him. She worked tirelessly to ensure he had food to eat and books to study from, yet her presence filled him with shame.

One day, during a school event, she visited him. The moment she stepped into the courtyard, Ajay's classmates erupted into cruel laughter. "Your mother looks like a monster!" they jeered.

Humiliated beyond measure, Ajay ran home that evening and confronted her. "Why did you come to my school? Why do you have to look like this? You are a disgrace!"

His mother said nothing. That night, when Ajay woke up for a drink of water, he found her sitting alone in the dimly lit kitchen, crying silently.

That was the moment Ajay decided—he would leave this life behind. He studied relentlessly, pushing himself toward success. Many years later, he found himself at the top—a high-paying job, a luxurious home, a beautiful wife, and a daughter who was the light of his life.

He never once thought of his mother.

Then, one day, on his daughter's birthday, a knock came at the door. As he opened it, his past stood before him.

His mother.

Aged, frail, yet standing with the same silent resilience.

Ajay's heart clenched. His guests whispered among themselves, their curious eyes fixed on the woman.

"Who is she?" someone asked.

Ajay, in his panic, declared, "I don't know who you are! You must have the wrong house!"

For a brief moment, pain flickered in his mother's weary eyes. Then, with a bow of her head, she softly replied, "Oh… I see. I must have made a mistake. I am sorry to have troubled you."

And she left.

Relieved, Ajay shut the door, silencing the remnants of his conscience.

Years passed. Then, one day, a letter arrived. A school reunion. On a whim, he decided to go.

After the event, curiosity led him back to his childhood home. The small, worn-down hut still stood, but it felt colder, emptier. Inside, on an old table, he found a letter.

It was from his mother.

'My son,

I think my time in this world is ending. I won't visit you again, for I know I have embarrassed you enough. But I wish, just once, I could have seen you one last time.

I am sorry for my appearance. I am sorry for my existence being a burden to you.

You see, when you were very young, you had an accident and lost an eye. As a mother, I could not bear the thought of you growing up incomplete, so I gave you mine.

The surgery left me scarred, but I was never sad about it. You were my world, and I was happy that through my eye, you could see life in its fullness.

Even though you hated me, I never stopped loving you. I was always proud of you, even from afar. I am sorry that I was not beautiful enough for you. I am sorry that I could not be the mother you wanted.

I love you, my son. I always have. I always will.

— Mother'

Ajay's world crumbled. He had spent his life despising the very person who had given him everything. The one eye he saw the world through—it was hers. And now, she was gone.

No apology could ever bring her back.

No regret could ever erase what he had done.

Shambav finished his tale.

The young man sitting beside him had turned pale, his hands shaking. His breath came in short gasps as he struggled to speak.

Tears streamed down his face, uncontrolled, raw.

And then, in that moment, realisation dawned upon him.

His mother, the one he had scorned, belittled, and abandoned—had she too made a sacrifice he had never known? Had she too given something up for him, something he never bothered to see?

Shambav's voice was gentle, yet firm.

"Never despise those who gave you life. Parents sacrifice silently, without expectation, without reward. Their love is not always spoken—it is stitched into the very fabric of our existence. And often, by the time we realise it, it is too late."

The young man sobbed, his body trembling with the weight of his newfound truth.

The devotees, too, were in tears.

And Sam, who had once questioned his master's silence, now understood. Some lessons cannot be taught by mere words or interventions. Some lessons must be lived, felt, and awakened from within.

As the sun dipped below the horizon, casting the sky in shades of crimson and gold, Shambav stood up and walked away.

For he knew—the seed had been planted. Now, it was up to the young man to let it grow.

Beyond Appearances

"Regret is the heaviest burden, for it carries the words we never said and the love we realised too late."

\- *Shree Shambav*

During one of his discourses, Shambav's serene voice filled the hall. The gathered disciples sat in quiet anticipation, absorbing every word.

Breaking the silence, Nita, one of the seekers, asked, "Master, why do people often judge and respect others based on their appearance?"

Shambav smiled, his eyes holding both warmth and depth. "Because the world is conditioned to see through the lens of materialism, mistaking the wrapping for the gift inside. Our eyes deceive us when our hearts are closed. Let me share a story."

The hall grew silent, and the devotees leaned in, eager for the lesson that would unfold.

In a bustling metropolis, a man with unkempt hair, sun-worn skin, and a weathered appearance walked into the grandest hotel in the city, holding his young daughter's hand. His clothes, patched in places, bore the marks of hard labor. The polished floors of the hotel seemed to reject the dust on his feet, and the chandeliers above cast a glow that made his presence feel even more out of place.

The guests and staff exchanged uneasy glances, silently questioning—How did this man enter here?

Yet, undeterred by the silent judgment, Ashwin, the father, found a table and seated his daughter, Medha. A waiter approached, his posture hesitant but professional, placing two gleaming glasses of water before them. With practiced politeness, he asked, "What would you like to order, sir?"

Ashwin's face lit up with pride as he gently stroked his daughter's hair. "I had promised my little girl that if she topped the state exams, I would bring her here to eat dosa. Today, she has fulfilled her promise. Now, it is my turn."

His voice carried no embarrassment—only pure, unfiltered love.

The waiter, taken aback, asked, "And for you, sir?"

Ashwin shook his head with a smile. "I only have money for one dosa. My daughter has many more milestones to reach, and I want her to enjoy this moment."

Something in the father's words stirred the waiter's soul. He walked straight to the manager and narrated the story, his voice trembling. "Sir, let me pay for their meal from my salary. I cannot let them leave like this."

The manager, deeply moved, took the story to the owner of the hotel. The owner, a man of wisdom, listened in silence before saying, "We will not just serve them a meal. We will celebrate this child's achievement as our own."

What happened next was beyond imagination. The hotel was transformed into a place of festivity. A table was specially decorated, and the entire staff gathered to honor Medha's success. The owner himself joined the celebration, personally serving the dosa to the young girl. Not only that, but sweets were packed and sent to her entire neighborhood, so the joy could spread far and wide.

Tears welled in Ashwin's eyes. Medha, overwhelmed by such unexpected kindness, held her father's hand tightly, as if anchoring herself to the moment.

Years passed.

The hotel continued to thrive, its values intact. One day, the owner received news that the district collector had chosen to have breakfast at their establishment. A special table was arranged, just as it had been years ago.

When the collector arrived, the entire staff stood in respect. The air held an unspoken reverence.

The collector, a poised and dignified woman, stepped forward, looked around, and then did something unexpected—she bowed before the hotel owner and the waiter who had once served her.

Her voice, steady yet emotional, rang through the hall. "Do you recognize me?"

Silence. The staff exchanged puzzled looks.

She smiled, her eyes glistening. "I am Medha—the same girl whose father once could only afford one dosa. That day, you did not just feed me; you fed my dreams, and my faith in humanity. You saw my worth beyond my father's tattered clothes. Today, I wish to repay you—not with money, but with the same kindness you showed me."

She turned to the staff and announced, "Today, every guest's meal will be on me. Because it was here, in this very place, that I learned the greatest lesson—not about success, but about humanity."

The hall erupted in applause. The hotel owner, humbled, simply placed his hand on Medha's head, as a father would.

Shambav looked at Nita with gentle eyes. "We must never be deceived by appearances, for the soul knows no dress, no riches, no outward beauty. Every human being is a story unfolding, a purpose waiting to be fulfilled. Respect is not about status—it is about recognising the light in another, even when the world fails to see it."

Tears welled in Nita's eyes. The lesson had reached not just her ears, but her heart.

The Infinite Reservoir of Love

"Love is not measured by how much we receive, but by how deeply we give. The echo of true love is not in words spoken, but in hearts touched."

- *Shree Shambav*

In a quiet village cradled between the arms of the mountains, there lived an old woman named Radha. She owned no riches, no titles, no land, yet she was the wealthiest soul in the village. Her wealth was not counted in gold or silver, but in the warmth of her embrace, the gentleness of her words, and the boundless love she gave so freely.

Children flocked to her like birds returning to their nests, drawn by the magnetic pull of her kindness. She told stories that made their hearts dance, and when she laughed, it was as if the wind itself carried her joy through the village. Even the elders, burdened by life's weariness, found solace in her presence.

One evening, a young man named Arjun stood on the cliffs overlooking the village. His heart was a barren wasteland, stripped of joy by years of disappointment, fear, and sorrow. His mind was a restless sea, churning with unanswered questions. As he stood in silence, his gaze fell upon Radha.

She was playing with the village children, her laughter rising into the evening sky like a melody. It was pure, unguarded, infectious. The children, caught in its spell, laughed with her, their voices intertwining in a symphony of unfiltered joy.

Something inside Arjun stirred. Without realising it, he smiled—then chuckled—then laughed, a deep, liberating laugh that shook loose the heaviness in his soul. In that fleeting moment, he felt something he hadn't in years: peace.

But as the laughter faded, an unease crept back into him. How? he wondered. How could an old woman, who had seen the trials of life, carry such lightness? Had she never known pain? Had she never suffered? Was she untouched by loss?

That night, sleep eluded him. He lay awake, staring at the ever-moving clouds, searching for answers in their restless dance.

The next morning, he sought Radha. When he found her, he asked, "Radha Ma, how do you love so much? How are you so happy? My heart is hollow, and I feel nothing but emptiness. How can I learn to love like you?"

Radha smiled, her eyes reflecting lifetimes of wisdom. She took his hand in hers, wrinkled yet firm, and said, "Let me tell you a story."

The Seeker of Eternal Happiness

Long ago, in a distant kingdom, there was a king who had everything—power, wealth, a grand palace—but he was not happy. He spent his days in search of something he could not name, an ache he could not soothe. He summoned sages, read scriptures, and travelled across lands, yet nothing filled the void inside him.

One day, he heard of a wise hermit who lived deep within a forest, a man said to hold the secret of eternal happiness. With great hope, the king rode through the wilderness, finally reaching the hermit, who sat beneath an ancient banyan tree.

Falling to his knees, the king pleaded, "Wise one, I have everything, yet I feel nothing. I am empty. Can you teach me the secret of eternal happiness?"

The hermit opened his eyes, deep and knowing, and said, "To find eternal happiness, you must first fill your own heart with love. Only then will joy cease to be something you seek and become something you are."

The king frowned. "But how do I fill my heart with love?"

The hermit smiled. "Sit with yourself. Learn to see yourself not as a king, but as a being worthy of love—not for what you have or what you do, but for who you are. When you embrace your own soul with kindness, love will no longer be something you give—it will be something you overflow with. That is the secret of eternal happiness."

The king returned to his palace and did as the hermit advised. At first, it was difficult. He was accustomed to seeking approval from others, but he had never sought love from within. Over time, something changed. He no longer looked to his kingdom for happiness; he found it within himself. His heart, once a locked chamber, became an open garden, and in its bloom, he became a source of joy for his people.

Radha placed a hand on Arjun's shoulder. "You see, my child, you cannot give what you do not have. A river does not ask where to flow—it flows because it is full. Love is the same. If you feel empty, it is because you have forgotten to love yourself."

Arjun lowered his gaze. "But how do I love myself?"

Radha's voice softened. "Live your life with what you have, but do not be bound by it. Every bondage is suffering. Be in the world, but not weighed down by it. Learn to be detached yet deeply connected. And then, love will not be something you seek—it will be something you are."

Arjun sat in silence, her words sinking into the depths of his soul. He realised that all his life, he had sought love outside himself, hoping others would fill the emptiness he felt. But love, true love, was never something to be found—it was something to be awakened.

And so, his journey inward began.

As the days turned to weeks, he saw himself with new eyes. He recognised his worth, not in achievements or accolades, but in his existence itself. The more he embraced himself, the lighter he felt. And one day, he laughed—not because of Radha, not because of anyone else, but because joy had finally found a home within him.

Shambav said, "Just like Arjun, when you find love within yourself, you transform. Your love ceases to be a transaction and becomes a gift. That is true love—being love, gift-love—flowing freely, expecting nothing, yet enriching everything it touches. And in this love, you will not only find joy but the fulfilment of your deepest self."

A hushed silence fell over the disciples. Some closed their eyes, letting the wisdom settle within. Others smiled, as if a long-lost truth had finally been remembered.

Shambav whispered, "Love is not something to be acquired—it is something to be realised. And when you find it within yourself, the world will no longer be a place you seek love from, but a place you pour love into."

The Lost River

"You are not a single drop lost in the sea; you are the entire ocean, longing to remember itself. The vastness you seek is not outside of you—it is within, waiting to be found."

- *Shree Shambav*

After a long journey through winding paths and sunlit meadows, Shambav and his devotees finally arrived at a tranquil grove. Beneath the vast embrace of an ancient banyan tree, they found rest. A cool breeze whispered through the branches, carrying the scent of damp earth and fallen leaves. Their exhaustion melted as they sat in quiet reflection, the weight of their travels easing into the stillness of the moment.

After their meal, they took a brief respite, the rhythm of their breath syncing with the soft rustling of leaves above them. When they awoke, they strolled through the sacred grove, their hearts lightened by the serenity surrounding them.

As Shambav settled once more beneath the tree, his devotees gathered around him.

A devotee named Akshatha broke the silence, her voice tinged with longing.

"Master," she asked, "how do we return to our true source? The world is filled with so many beliefs, traditions, and paths. How do we know which way is right?"

Shambav's gaze softened, and a gentle smile played on his lips. "Ah, Akshatha," he murmured. "Let me tell you a story."

The Journey of the River

Once, high in the embrace of the mountains, a river was born—a mere trickle at first, fragile as a whispered prayer. She danced over stones, glistening in the sunlight, singing a song only the wind understood. As she tumbled downward, she grew stronger, her currents deepening, carving valleys and nourishing forests.

She loved her journey, the way she shaped the land, the way she cradled life within her depths. But as she flowed further, she began to forget where she had come from.

One day, she reached the edge of a vast desert. The golden sands stretched endlessly before her, their silence pressing against the roar of her waters. For the first time, fear gripped her heart.

"What lies beyond this desert?" she wondered. "If I cross it, will I vanish? Will I cease to exist?"

She hesitated, uncertain of her next step. And so she sought answers.

She first met a sage meditating by her banks.

"O wise one," she asked, "what is my destiny?"

The sage smiled. "You seek the ocean," he said, "but you fear losing yourself. The ocean is not the end—it is the beginning. You are not separate from it. You are the ocean in another form."

The river trembled. "But I have spent my whole life as a river. If I surrender, will I still be me?"

The sage chuckled and returned to his meditation, leaving her with more questions than before.

She continued her journey and arrived at a village where people spoke of a great kingdom beyond the desert.

"There is a land where the Creator awaits us," an old woman told her. "If you are faithful, you will be welcomed into His eternal embrace."

The river hesitated. "But what of the ocean?"

The old woman shook her head. "The ocean is empty. The kingdom is full."

Still unsure, the river flowed onward.

Further along, she met a weary traveller, his gaze fixed upon the distant horizon.

"Life is suffering," he said, his voice carrying the weight of countless roads walked. "We flow, we crash, we evaporate, and we return—all because we are bound by longing. If you wish to be free, you must cease to flow altogether. Let the thirst of the desert swallow you. Let the sun take you. Then, you will no longer be bound."

The river trembled. "But what will I become?"

The traveller only smiled.

Carrying these voices within her, the river reached the desert's edge, where silence stretched beyond thought.

The Surrender

The sun beat down upon her waters, and she felt herself begin to wane. The more she resisted, the more she fragmented. Her existence, which once felt so strong and certain, now seemed to slip through her grasp.

And then, a whisper rose with the wind.

"Do not resist."

The river stilled.

"Let go," the voice murmured, "and you will see."

With a trembling breath, the river surrendered.

She lifted into the sky, no longer bound by her form, rising as mist into the embrace of the heavens. She drifted across vast distances, weightless, free. And then, as if guided by an ancient memory, she was drawn back to the mountains. She fell once more as rain, kissing the earth, becoming a stream, flowing once again toward the sea.

And at last, she understood.

She had never been lost. She had never truly disappeared. She had always been the ocean—whether as a river, as mist, or as rain.

The ocean was not the end.

It was home.

As Shambav's voice faded, a hush fell over the devotees. The story settled deep within them, like rain sinking into the parched earth.

Akshatha wiped away a tear she hadn't realised had fallen.

"So," she whispered, "no matter which path we take—whether we seek Nirvana, Moksha, Heaven, or peace—we all return?"

Shambav nodded. "Yes, Akshatha. Some take lifetimes. Some take moments. Some dissolve like a wave, others stand in the light of the Divine. But in the end, the journey is the same.

"We do not disappear.

"We return."

The Tender Heart

"True love does not cling, demand, or possess—it flows like a river, nourishing everything in its path, yet never asking the land to hold it captive."

- *Shree Shambav*

After a long journey, Shambav and his devotees settled near a flowing river beneath the sheltering arms of an ancient tree. The cool, rhythmic murmur of the water harmonised with the rustling leaves, creating a sanctuary of peace. After freshening up in the flowing river and nourishing themselves with a handful of wild fruits, they rested for a while. As the golden hues of the setting sun painted the sky, Shambav began his discourse.

Roopa, her eyes filled with curiosity, asked, "Master, what is the difference between kindness, compassion, and empathy?"

Shambav smiled gently, his gaze lingering on the river that meandered through the valley. "Roopa," he began, "let me share a story with you."

The Nest of Compassion

Deep within a sacred forest, where the trees whispered ancient secrets and the winds carried forgotten songs, an old monk wandered, his heart attuned to the rhythms of nature. As he walked, his eyes were drawn to a magnificent nest perched high atop a sturdy tree—a masterpiece woven by the delicate hands of the mother bird.

His soul stirred by its beauty, the monk approached a young shepherd boy who was tending his flock nearby. With an affectionate smile, he offered the boy two silver coins in exchange for the nest, eager to possess its delicate splendour. But the boy, with the clarity of an untainted heart, refused without hesitation.

The monk, undeterred, increased his offer to five silver coins, convinced that the boy would not resist such wealth. Yet, the boy remained resolute, his small hands clutching his crook as he gazed into the monk's wise yet longing eyes.

With a voice steady yet soft, the boy said, "Sir, within that nest, fragile lives rest beneath their mother's wings. To take it would be to steal not just twigs and feathers, but the comfort of a mother's embrace, the sanctuary of innocence. No amount of silver can outweigh such sorrow."

A breeze stirred the leaves, and with it, something stirred within the monk's heart. In that moment, he saw with sudden clarity—the boy, though young and unlearned in the ways of the world, understood something far greater than wisdom alone. He understood the language of the heart, the depth of compassion that transcends mere knowledge.

With reverence, the monk bowed to the boy, placing the five silver coins in his hand—not as payment, but as an offering to the wisdom he had just received. As he walked away, his feet felt lighter, his heart unburdened by longing. He realised that true wisdom is not in the accumulation of knowledge but in the ability to feel deeply, to understand another's pain as one's own.

The River's Reflection

Shambav paused, allowing the story's essence to settle in the hearts of his devotees. He then turned to Roopa and continued, "You see, kindness, compassion, and empathy are like different currents of the same river."

Kindness is when you see someone thirsty and offer them a drink—it is an act of goodwill, simple yet beautiful. Compassion is when you see someone thirsty, and you not only offer them water but sit beside them, ensuring they are comforted, understanding that their suffering is also yours. But empathy is when you feel their thirst as if it were your own, when their suffering does not merely exist outside of you but within you, moving you to act not out of duty, but from the depths of your own heart."

The river before them gurgled softly, as if whispering its own wisdom. "A river," Shambav continued, "does not ask who deserves its water. It flows freely, nourishing all who come to its banks. Yet, a river also knows its source—it does not give until it has filled itself first. That is how we must love. To be kind is noble, to be compassionate is divine, but to be truly empathetic is to dissolve the boundaries between oneself and the world."

Roopa lowered her gaze, absorbing the depth of his words. The devotees sat in silence, their souls stirred like the ripples on the river's surface. Shambav's voice was soft yet resolute as he concluded, "The greatest wisdom is not found in books, nor in debates of intellect, but in a heart that feels, a heart that understands without words, and gives without conditions."

A single leaf drifted onto the river, carried effortlessly by the current. Watching it, Roopa felt something shift within her. The answer had always been there, flowing like the river—waiting to be seen, waiting to be understood.

Beneath the Whispering Willow

"Even the longest night cannot prevent the dawn. Even in sorrow, there is a light within you—waiting, patient, ready to rise."

- *Shree Shambav*

Shambav and his devotees journeyed through a village cradled in the embrace of towering mountains, where the air carried the scent of blooming jasmine, and the trees stood like silent sentinels of time. Birds sang in playful symphony, and the river nearby hummed an eternal lullaby.

One of the devotees, Kiran, observed the villagers with curiosity. Their faces bore the ease of contentment, their laughter unburdened, their lives seemingly untouched by the turmoil that plagued so many.

"Master," Kiran asked, "why do these people seem so peaceful and happy?"

His curiosity deepened, and he approached a villager, an old man weaving a basket under the shade of a banyan tree. "Sir," Kiran inquired, "what is the secret to this village's harmony?"

The old man smiled, his eyes crinkling like parchment folded by time. "Whenever we are troubled, we seek the wise one who lives by the riverbank. His words have the power to soothe even the weariest soul."

Intrigued, Kiran and the devotees followed the winding path to the river, where they saw an elderly man laughing, his voice mingling with the giggles of children playing around him. His presence felt like a balm, radiating warmth that reached even the most silent corners of the heart.

Kiran, unable to contain his curiosity, stepped forward. "Wise one, how do you keep this village at peace?"

The old man chuckled, his laughter as light as the river breeze. "Young man," he said, "it is the power of words."

Kiran frowned, expecting something more elaborate. He simply nodded and rejoined the devotees, yet the old man's words lingered in his mind. That night, as the moon draped its silver veil over the village, he lay awake, restless with questions. How could mere words heal pain, dissolve suffering, and bring lasting peace?

At sunrise, the devotees gathered beneath the shade of a great tree, where Shambav began his discourse.

Kiran, still haunted by the old man's response, finally voiced his thoughts. "Master, how can words possess such power? How can they remove suffering and bring happiness?"

Shambav smiled, his gaze deep as the sky before a storm. "Let me tell you a story…"

In a village not unlike this one, a young girl named Amelia was drawn to the great willow tree at its edge. Its branches swayed as if whispering the wisdom of forgotten ages, its roots anchored in stories long past. Beneath its shelter, she found solace, but one day, she stumbled upon something unexpected—a small, rusted box hidden among the roots.

With trembling hands, she opened it and found old letters, their parchment yellowed with time, their words carrying echoes of lost voices.

The first letter was from a woman named Isabella:

"I have lost my husband, and each day feels like an eternity of emptiness. How do I find the strength to move forward when my heart still aches for him?"

Amelia's heart clenched. Though she could not fully grasp Isabella's grief, she felt an overwhelming urge to comfort her. She wrote back in careful strokes:

"Dear Isabella, your husband's love is not gone—it lives in your laughter, in the kindness you share, in the memories that time cannot steal. The willow bends in the storm but never breaks. Let its strength be yours."

She placed her response back in the box, unsure if it would ever reach its intended soul. Days passed, and to her astonishment, she found another letter waiting for her—a message of gratitude from Isabella, her words infused with newfound hope.

Thus, Amelia became the silent guardian of the willow's letters.

One by one, the villagers sought solace in the unseen confidant beneath the willow.

A young man named James wrote:

"I am drowning in my family's expectations. They wish for me to be something I am not. How do I break free?"

Amelia replied:

"Dear James, the river does not ask the mountain which way to flow. It carves its own path, trusting the journey. Follow your heart, for it knows the way."

James, emboldened, finally spoke his truth. He pursued his passion for painting, and in doing so, discovered not only himself but also a community that cherished his art.

Then came a letter from Richard, an aging father abandoned by his children:

"I gave them everything, yet they have forgotten me. Was I a bad father?"

Tears blurred Amelia's vision as she wrote:

"Dear Richard, the willow loses its leaves each winter but never grieves their departure—it knows that spring will bring new life. Love given is never wasted. Open your heart, and new connections will find their way to you."

Richard, once drowning in loneliness, found new companionship among the villagers, forming bonds he never thought possible.

Over time, the letters beneath the willow became a sacred ritual, a quiet sanctuary where souls found solace. It was never about giving perfect answers—it was about listening, about offering words woven with care, about making someone feel seen.

One evening, Amelia discovered a letter addressed to her:

"To the one who replies, thank you. Your words have been the lantern in my darkest night. You have reminded me that I am never truly alone."

She placed a hand on the tree's weathered bark, feeling its steady pulse beneath her fingertips. The wisdom she had given to others had come full circle, echoing back to her.

With a whisper to the willow, she murmured, "Even in the darkest times, a single kind word can be the flicker of light that saves a soul."

The Power of Words

As Shambav finished the story, the devotees sat in a profound silence.

Kiran's voice was barely above a whisper. "So… words do more than speak. They hold, they heal, they save."

Shambav nodded. "Words, when spoken with intention, are not just sounds. They are threads that weave together the fabric of human connection. They can wound like a blade or mend like a healer's touch. They can imprison or set free. They can turn sorrow into solace, despair into hope."

A gentle breeze rustled through the trees, carrying his words into the vast sky.

"The wise old man," Kiran murmured, realisation dawning on him. "That's what he meant by the power of words."

Shambav smiled. "Yes, Kiran. Sometimes, all a weary heart needs is to be heard, to be acknowledged. To know that they are not alone."

Kiran looked toward the river, where the old man still played with the children, his laughter as light as the morning sun. He had carried the village's burdens, not with grand gestures or profound philosophies, but with the simplest, most powerful gift of all—words spoken with love.

As they sat beneath the vast sky, the devotees realised the profound truth of Shambav's story.

The power of words was not in their sound.

It was in the souls they touched.

TWENTY + ONE

The Unheard Symphony

"To hold on to the past is to grip a blade; the tighter you cling, the deeper the wound. Freedom is not in forgetting, but in learning to carry memories with open hands."

- *Shree Shambav*

In a tranquil village cradled by towering mountains and whispering trees, the morning air carried the scent of earth and the soft melodies of a nearby riverlet. Birds sang their morning hymns, and butterflies danced like floating fragments of light. The world seemed wrapped in an unbroken serenity, but not far from where Shambav and his devotees strolled through the dew-kissed meadows, a lone figure sat in silence, weighed down by an invisible burden.

John, one of Shambav's followers, observed the young man from afar. There was something about his posture—a quiet fragility, a sadness that clung to him like the mist in the valley. As John approached, he felt the ache that lay beneath the silence.

Gently, he asked, "Why do you sit here, heavy with sorrow, when the world around you sings with life?"

The young man, named Mark, looked up with tired eyes. His voice, though steady, carried the echoes of something broken.

"I was once an artist," he said, staring at his calloused hands. "I breathed life into clay, shaping beauty from dust. My ceramic pottery was admired, my hands danced with purpose. But one day, fate struck without warning—I met with an accident. I survived, yet I am not the man I was. Sleep escapes me, my hands tremble, my thoughts scatter like broken shards. My work no longer carries its former soul, and people no longer find beauty in what I create."

His words hung in the air like a lament carried by the wind.

John, moved by the depth of Mark's pain, placed a hand on his shoulder. "Mark, if you are willing, come with us to our discourse today. Perhaps, in silence, you may find the answer you seek."

Mark hesitated but then nodded. That evening, beneath the great banyan tree where wisdom often took root, the devotees gathered, their hearts open like pages waiting to be written upon. As the golden light of dusk bathed the earth, John turned to his Master.

"What is the power of silence? Why do people change so profoundly after an accident? What is this shift that overtakes them?"

Shambav, his gaze deep as the ocean, let the question settle in the quiet air before he spoke.

"Let me tell you a story…

There once was a gifted artist named Sophia. Her world was painted with melodies—the hum of the morning breeze, the rhythm of footsteps on cobbled streets, the laughter of children in the distance. Every brushstroke she laid upon the canvas was infused with the music that surrounded her.

Then, in a cruel twist of fate, an accident stole her hearing. In an instant, the world she knew fell silent. What was once a symphony became a hollow, unbroken void. Her studio, once alive with inspiration, became a tomb of quiet despair. The brushes lay untouched, the canvases blank, as she struggled to find meaning in a life where the music had ceased.

Yet, amid this silence, there was Sam—a friend who had walked beside her since childhood. He saw not only her sorrow but also the untapped depths of her spirit.

One day, he visited her, notebook in hand, and wrote:

'I miss you, Sophia. Can we talk?'

She hesitated before replying:

'I don't know if I can do this, Sam. Everything is different now.'

But Sam was patient. He didn't attempt to fill the silence with empty words. Instead, he showed her that sound was not the only language of the world. He took her on long walks where they observed life in its rawest form—the way light stretched over rooftops, the way leaves trembled under the weight of the wind, the way laughter carried across a room even if she couldn't hear it.

One day, at an art gallery, Sophia stood before a painting that pulsed with vibrant colour. She could feel it. The movement, the emotion, the energy woven into every stroke.

Sam handed her the notebook.

'What do you see?' he wrote.

She hesitated, then replied, 'I see motion, emotions. The colors are singing.'

Sam smiled.

'Exactly. Art is not just about hearing. It is about feeling. Silence is its own kind of symphony.'

That night, Sophia returned to her studio. She picked up her brush for the first time in months. But this time, she didn't listen for music—she felt it. Her art transformed. Without sound, she found depth in light and shadow, in the unspoken conversations of colours. She painted emotions that resonated beyond words.

One by one, people came to see her work. They didn't need to hear music to understand the stories within her paintings. They felt them. And in that moment, Sophia understood—she had not lost her gift. She had simply found a new way to express it."

Shambav looked at Mark, his voice gentle but firm.

"Life does not take without also giving. Silence does not signify emptiness—it is space for something new to emerge. Mark, perhaps your hands tremble because they are not meant to create as they once did, but in a new way. Your art is not lost; it is simply waiting to be reborn."

Tears welled in Mark's eyes. He had spent so long mourning what was gone that he had never considered what could still be created.

As the sun dipped below the horizon, the air was filled with the hum of quiet understanding. And beneath that vast sky, Mark held onto something he hadn't felt in a long time—hope.

The Forgotten Roots

"The greatest sorrow is not losing a parent, but realising too late that you never truly cherished them while they were still there."

\- *Shree Shambav*

Shree Shambav and his devoted followers walked through the vast, emerald meadows, the golden sunlight casting long shadows on the earth. The breeze carried the scent of wildflowers, and the sound of rustling leaves filled the air with a serene melody. As they journeyed, one of his devotees, Arjun, walked beside him, lost in deep thought. After a long silence, he finally spoke.

"Guruji, why do children neglect their parents in their old age? Do they not regret their actions?" His voice carried both curiosity and pain.

Shree Shambav sighed, his gaze soft but knowing. "Ah, Arjun," he said, "the heart of a child is pure when born, filled with love and gratitude. But as they grow, the world whispers illusions of self-importance, ambition, and independence. In the pursuit of success, they begin to believe they have risen alone, forgetting the roots that nurtured them."

Arjun listened intently as Shree Shambav continued, "Let me tell you a story."

In a small village, there lived a man named Raghav and his wife, Meera. They had a son, Karan, whom they loved beyond measure. Raghav was a simple farmer, and Meera stitched clothes to support the family. They lived modestly, but they gave Karan everything he needed—education, love, and values.

Karan grew up to be a brilliant young man. His parents worked tirelessly, sacrificing their comforts, eating less on some days, just to ensure he could study in a prestigious city college. When he graduated with honours and secured a high-paying job, Raghav and Meera's eyes welled with pride.

Karan moved to the city and got absorbed in his work. Initially, he called his parents often, but over time, the calls became infrequent, the visits rare. He started seeing their simple way of life as outdated, their presence as a disturbance in his busy world. He felt they would not understand his struggles, his ambitions, his lifestyle.

Years passed. Raghav and Meera waited at the doorstep, hoping for their son's return. Festivals came and went, but their home remained silent. Letters were written but never answered. They longed to see him, to hear his voice, to simply know he was happy.

One day, Raghav fell gravely ill. Meera, with trembling hands, wrote a letter to Karan, pleading with him to come home. But Karan was busy. His career was at its peak, and he convinced himself that he would visit once things settled down.

One evening, he received a phone call. A voice on the other end spoke words that shattered his world—his father had passed away. Guilt gripped his soul like a vice. He rushed to his village, his heart heavy with regret. When he reached his childhood home, he found his mother sitting alone, frail and grieving. The house, once filled with warmth, now seemed cold and empty.

Meera looked at him, her eyes full of unspoken pain. "Your father waited for you till his last breath, Karan. He used to sit outside every evening, hoping you would return. He never complained, never blamed you. He only wished to see his son one last time."

Tears streamed down Karan's face as he fell to his knees. "I was so blinded by my success that I forgot the ones who made it possible," he whispered. He realised that while he had been running after wealth and recognition, he had lost the most precious treasures of all—his parents' love and time with them.

Shree Shambav turned to Arjun, his voice gentle but firm. "Regret is a cruel teacher, my child. By the time it arrives, the lessons it brings are of no use. Success is a beautiful journey, but if you leave behind the hands that lifted you when you stumbled, then no achievement will ever bring true joy."

Arjun wiped a tear from his eye. "How can one ensure they never forget their parents, Guruji?"

Shree Shambav smiled. "Gratitude. Never let a day pass without expressing your love. Call them, visit them, listen to them. Make them feel valued, for they are the true reason behind your success. And remember, no wealth, no achievement, no recognition in the world can replace the warmth of a mother's hug or the pride in a father's eyes."

The devotees walked in silence, each absorbing the profound lesson in their hearts. The meadows stretched endlessly ahead, much like the path of life—filled with opportunities, but also choices. And the greatest choice one could make was never to leave behind those who had given them everything.

The Silent Echoes of an Empty Soul

"True fulfillment is not found in riches or power but in the love, purpose, and wisdom we nurture within."

- *Shree Shambav*

As the golden sun dipped below the horizon, painting the sky with hues of orange and crimson, Shambav and his devotees traversed a lush green meadow. The soft whispers of the wind wove through the swaying grass, carrying the scent of wildflowers and earth. Birds glided gracefully above, their silhouettes cutting through the fading light. It was in this tranquil setting that Padma, a devoted seeker, broke the contemplative silence.

"Guruji," she asked, her voice carrying both curiosity and longing, "Why is it that even those who are rich and powerful still feel empty? They have everything one could desire, yet their hearts remain restless."

Shambav paused, gazing at the vast expanse before him. He smiled gently, he gestured toward an old, mighty tree standing alone in the meadow.

"Do you see that tree, Padma?" he asked. "Its roots run deep beneath the earth, unseen but essential. The branches stretch towards the sky, seeking light, yet without strong roots, the tree would wither despite the abundance of sunlight."

Padma nodded, listening intently as Shambav continued.

"A person may possess wealth, status, and power—these are like the sunlight that nourishes the outer world. But if their soul is not deeply rooted in purpose, love, and truth, they will feel empty, no matter how much they have. They chase after things that sparkle, mistaking them for fulfilment."

A silence settled among the group, each devotee lost in contemplation. Then, Shambav shared a story, his voice carrying the weight of a lesson meant for the heart.

"Once, there was a great king, renowned for his wealth and dominion over vast lands. His palace was adorned with gold, his chambers filled with rare jewels, and his name echoed across kingdoms. Yet, every night, he lay awake, staring at the ceiling, unable to find rest. He could command armies, build monuments, and bestow riches upon his subjects, but he could not command peace within his own soul.

One day, he called upon a wise sage and asked, 'Why do I feel this void within me? I have everything the world could offer.' The sage smiled and handed him a simple clay pot. 'Fill this pot with water,' he instructed.

The king, puzzled, poured water into the pot. To his surprise, the water seeped out through a small crack at the bottom. No matter how much he poured, the pot would not hold the water.

The sage then said, 'Your heart is like this pot. You fill it with riches, power, and pleasures, yet it leaks because it lacks the foundation of true fulfilment. Only love, purpose, and selflessness can seal this crack and hold the waters of peace.'"

Padma sighed deeply, understanding the essence of the tale. "Then, Guruji, how can one find true fulfilment?"

Shambav smiled, his eyes gleaming with warmth. "True fulfilment comes not from what you accumulate, but from what you give. Love without expectation, serve without pride, and seek wisdom without arrogance. The greatest treasure lies not in gold or jewels, but in the depth of one's heart."

Life Coach and Philanthropist

Shree Shambav is the visionary founder of the Shree Shambav Ayur Rakshita Foundation (www.shambav-ayurrakshita.org). He founded this institution with a lofty goal: to recognise human identity across gender, ethnicity, and nationality. Through this organisation, he wants to assist all communities in realising their full potential and the intrinsic beauty of life.

Shree Shambav, a Life Coach, is dedicated to supporting people on their journeys of self-discovery and empowerment. He assists people in discovering who they are, determining what inspires and drives them, and overcoming limiting ideas. His approach clarifies what one wants in life, assisting people through goal-setting and a step-by-step process for achieving them. He empowers people to make deliberate and responsible decisions, allowing them to identify their blind spots and evolve as individuals via the use of numerous strategies and tools.

The foundation's bold, uncompromising, and compassionate ventures are always aimed at initiating the "Inner Transformation" process. They focus on spiritual growth, personal growth, and self-healing while emphasising that true progress lies in "Inclusive Growth and Co-existence." This philosophy drives all their initiatives, encouraging a holistic approach to development and well-being.

Under Shree Shambav's leadership, the foundation has launched several impactful movements:

Shree Shambav Green Movement: This mission is to create a healthy, green, and clean earth through responsible water conservation and greening initiatives. The movement strives to make the world a green paradise by encouraging sustainable living and environmental responsibility.

Shree Shambav Vidya Vedhika (Vizhuthugal): This project aims to help students and children by offering training, books, stationery, and uniforms. It aims to provide the next generation with the tools and resources they need to excel both academically and personally.

Shree Shambav and his foundation exemplify the spirit of compassion, transformation, and inclusive growth via their work, which has a profound impact on individuals and communities around the world. His work exemplifies the power of acknowledging and nourishing the human spirit, creating a world in which everyone can reach their full potential and appreciate the beauty of life.

TESTIMONIALS

Journey of Soul - Karma - "We die in our twenties and are buried at eighty." Remember that nothing can stop someone who refuses to be stopped. "Most people do not fail; they simply give up." Shree Shambav deserves full credit. It allowed me to sit and consider what I might miss out on in life. The author has delved into every aspect of our daily lives. How can a seemingly insignificant change in these seemingly insignificant details bring us such joy? The Soul of Journey teaches you the "art of living" as well as the "art of dying."

Twenty + One Series - The rich cultural heritage offered a host in twenty + one short stories with incredible imagination, morals and values prevalent at a given time, influencing how people respond to a crisis or any situation. The author has recreated images with universal values and morals. The plentiful of fascinating from faraway lands would leave the modern play and story writers a cringe. The book supports trust and immeasurable values instilling hope for the new generations.

Death - "Shree Shambav's 'Death - Light of Life and the Shadow of Death' is an extraordinary masterpiece that delves deep into the profound questions surrounding our existence and mortality. The book's opening statement, 'Nothing ever truly dies; it simply ceases to exist in one form before resuming it in another,' sets the stage for a thought-provoking exploration of death's multifaceted nature. Shambav's remarkable ability to navigate the philosophical complexities of death and our universal fear of it is both enlightening and comforting. This book is a testament to the power of understanding and acceptance."

Whispers of Eternity - "Reading 'Whispers of Eternity' by Shree Shambav was a transformative experience that left me captivated from beginning to end. Each section of this exquisite collection delves into the myriad facets of existence, offering poignant reflections on life, death, and everything in between. Shree Shambav's verses are a testament to the beauty of language and the power of expression, inviting readers to embark on a journey of self-discovery and spiritual awakening. Whether celebrating life's simple joys or grappling with the complexities of human emotion, this book is a timeless companion that speaks to the heart and soul of every reader."

Life Changing Journey Series - "Life Changing Journey Series II Inspirational Quotes" is a remarkable collection that illuminates the path to self-discovery and personal growth. With its inspiring quotes and insightful reflections, this book serves as a beacon of light in a world often shrouded in darkness. Each quote offers wisdom, guidance, and encouragement, reminding readers of their inner strength and resilience. A must-read for anyone seeking inspiration and enlightenment.

Learn To Love Yourself – "A Heartfelt Guide to Authentic Self-Love." "Learn to Love Yourself" invites readers on a transformative journey to embrace their true essence in a world often focused on external validation. Through ten insightful chapters, it gently reveals principles of genuine self-love, guiding readers to deepen their connection with themselves. Beyond surface positivity, it encourages the cultivation of resilient self-acceptance, from embracing one's unique qualities to setting empowering boundaries. With inspiring stories and practical wisdom, this book is a trusted companion on the path to inner peace, fulfilment, and joy, helping readers build lives that reflect their authentic selves.

The Power of Letting Go – This book has been a gift to my spiritual journey. Shree Shambav's insights into attachment, personal growth cycles, and forgiveness are enlightening. The concept of seven-year cycles resonated with me, helping me understand the natural phases of life. I feel more empowered to let go of what no longer serves me and step into a life of freedom and fulfilment. A truly beautiful read!

A Journey of Lasting Peace – "A Journey of Lasting Peace" feels like a trusted friend guiding you through the maze of self-discovery. The 18 transformative principles are both practical and deeply resonant, addressing everything from gratitude practices to the art of letting go. Each chapter is infused with warmth and wisdom, making it easy to apply the concepts to my life. I particularly appreciated the emphasis on physical health's connection to mental well-being; it served as a wake-up call for me to prioritize my health. This book is an invaluable resource for anyone serious about personal growth!

Astrology Unveiled Series – "Profound, Logical, and Inspiring". What stands out in Astrology Unveiled is the author's dedication to making Vedic astrology logical and approachable. Each concept flows naturally into the next, backed by examples and exercises. The insights into karma and life cycles add a philosophical depth rarely seen in astrology books. Perfect for anyone seeking spiritual growth alongside astrological knowledge!

The Entitlement Trap - "Thought-Provoking and Challenging" The book challenges readers to confront their own sense of entitlement, and that's not easy—but it's essential. The Entitlement Trap doesn't offer a one-size-fits-all approach. Instead, it's a thoughtful, layered examination of how entitlement can limit our growth. The chapter on "Defining Your Own Hill" was particularly impactful, as it pushed me to reconsider which challenges are truly worth pursuing. A thought-provoking read for those willing to do the inner work to create a life they can be proud of.

Whispers of a Dying Soul – "A Soul-Stirring Reflection on Life's Unspoken Truths" **-** *Whispers of a Dying Soul: Unspoken Regrets and Unlived Dreams"* is a deeply moving exploration of the unexpressed emotions and unfulfilled aspirations that shape our lives in ways we often don't realise. This book invites readers to confront the powerful, often hidden impact of regret while guiding them through a journey of introspection and healing. Each page opens a space to reflect on the choices that define us—from moments of unspoken love to neglected passions—offering a gentle reminder to live authentically and courageously.

Whispers of the Soul: A Journey Through Haiku - is a mesmerising collection that speaks directly to the heart. Each haiku is a delicate brushstroke capturing life's fleeting beauty and timeless wisdom, inviting readers into moments of deep reflection and peace. This book is a balm for the soul, guiding us to find meaning in stillness and connection in simplicity. The themes of nature, love, and mindfulness echo universal truths, resonating with quiet, powerful grace. It's a book to be savoured slowly, cherished deeply, and returned to often. Truly, a gift for anyone seeking calm and clarity in life's chaos.

Whispers of Silence - Unlocking Inner Power through Stillness by Shree Shambav is a rare gem that beckons readers to pause, reflect, and reconnect with their inner selves. In a world that never stops talking, this book offers a profound exploration of silence—not as a void but as a rich and transformative space.

From the first page, Shree Shambav's writing resonates deeply, blending scientific insights with spiritual wisdom in a way that feels both universal and deeply personal. The author's ability to bridge the tangible and the transcendent makes this book an invaluable guide for anyone navigating the chaos of modern life.

The Power of Words: Transforming Speech, Transforming Lives - "The Power of Words is a profound and enlightening guide that has transformed the way I approach communication. Shree Shambav masterfully uncovers the hidden influence of our words on relationships, self-perception, and overall well-being. This book doesn't just teach you how to speak; it inspires mindful communication that fosters connection and trust. The insights on replacing negative patterns like gossip and judgment with kindness and authenticity are truly life-changing. The practical strategies and engaging narratives make it an invaluable resource for personal and professional growth. A must-read for anyone striving to communicate with intention, clarity, and compassion. Highly recommended!"

The Art of Intentional Living: Minimalism for a Life of Purpose - "The Art of Intentional Living is a refreshing guide to finding clarity in a cluttered world. With practical wisdom and profound insights, it inspires you to simplify, prioritise, and live with purpose. A must-read for anyone seeking balance and fulfilment."

Awakening the Infinite: The Power of Consciousness in Transforming Life - "Awakening the Infinite is a transformative guide that expands the mind and nourishes the soul. With profound insights and practical wisdom, this book beautifully explores the power of consciousness, helping readers connect with their true purpose and inner potential. It is a journey of self-discovery, healing, and spiritual awakening, offering clarity and inspiration at every turn. A must-read for anyone looking to live with greater awareness, meaning, and authenticity."

Beyond the Veil Series: A Profound and Thought-Provoking Exploration - *"Beyond the Veil"* is a beautifully written book that dives deep into one of life's greatest mysteries—what happens after we die? The author does a remarkable job of balancing science, philosophy, and spirituality to provide an insightful and well-researched perspective. I especially appreciated the discussions on near-death experiences and consciousness beyond the body. This book has changed the way I perceive life and death, leaving me with a sense of peace and curiosity. Highly recommended for anyone seeking answers to life's deepest questions!

ACKNOWLEDGEMENTS

To my grandfathers, grandmothers, mothers, fathers, aunts, uncles, neighbours, sisters, brothers, friends, and teachers, they poured in endless moral stories, retellings of Ramayana, Mahabharata, Puranas, Upanishads, and so on.

My teachers, neighbours, and kindred souls. Who provided us with a stage to perform wonderful Puranic stories and were gracious enough to acknowledge our efforts.

The artists and translators of epics have served as a source of inspiration, invigorating our spirits, making these works accessible, and enabling us to grasp the profound depths and deeper dimensions they contain.

I also cherish the stimulating conversations; I had with my wonderful mothers, Punitha Muniswamy and Uma Devi.

Our family's youngest member, Aadhya, who always overwhelmed me with questions, inspired this book.

I would likewise prefer to express gratitude to Mr Sivakumar, Mrs Roopa Sivakumar, Mr Akshaya

Rajesh, Ms Akshatha Rajesh, Ms Apeksha Prabhu, Mr Akanksh Prabhu, Mr Nikash Sarasambi, Mrs Spoorthi Nikash for their valuable inputs.

I must thank Mr Rajesh, Mr Savan Prabhu, Mrs Revathi Rajesh, Mrs Rajani Sarasambi, and Mrs Manju Reshma, who encouraged me and often suggested writing a book. Their unwavering belief that I had something valuable to offer kept me going during my writing sessions.

Love you all,

Shree Shambav

www.shambav.org

shreeshambav@gmail.com

BOOKS BY – AUTHOR

Journey of Soul - KARMA

"Journey of Soul – Karma" is a heartfelt exploration of life's profound truths in our increasingly complex world. Addressing challenges, inequalities, and the quest for meaning, this book brings the timeless concept of Karma into focus. It emphasizes Karma not merely as philosophy, but as a guiding principle for our daily lives, inspiring us to walk a path of integrity and purpose. Through this journey, readers gain insights into how actions shape destinies, encouraging a life aligned with truth and compassion. It's a beacon for those seeking a deeper, more fulfilled existence.

Death - Light of Life and the Shadow of Death

In *Light of Life and the Shadow of Death*, the enigma of mortality is approached with clarity and compassion. Death is an inevitable certainty, yet it casts a lingering shadow of fear over our lives, stirring grief and despair as we strive to prolong our time on earth. This profound work examines the fate of departed souls and the heavy emotions we attach to loss. Yet, it offers a path toward accepting death and finding peace amid life's uncertainties. Exploring our origins, ethical values, and purpose, it unveils the sustaining truth of existence. The shadow of death, though daunting, is reframed as a shared, universal experience—one that calls us to confront our deepest fears with wisdom and grace.

Whispers of Eternity 150 Plus - A Symphony of Soulful Verses

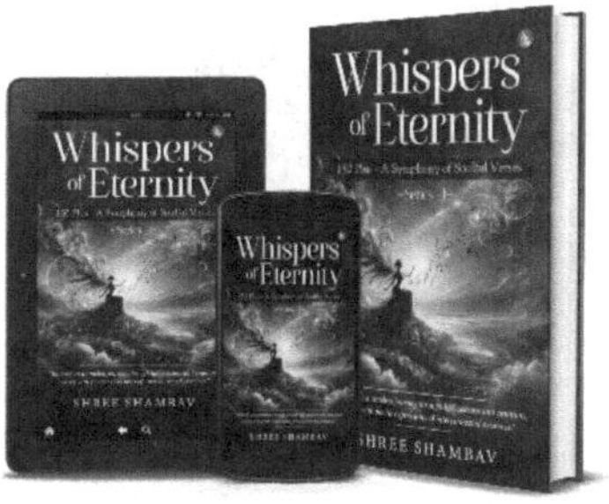

Step into the soul-stirring world of *Whispers of Eternity* by Shree Shambav, a collection of over 150 poems that capture the essence of the human experience. Divided into sections like "Through the Seasons," "Whispers of Hope," and "Threads of Unity," the book journeys through life's phases, emotions, and the universal connections that bind us all. Shree Shambav's verses touch upon nature, love, and spirituality, inspiring readers to find beauty in the everyday. Each poem is a finely crafted reflection, rich with insight and depth. *Whispers of Eternity* invites readers to pause, reflect, and embark on a timeless journey through the landscapes of the heart and soul.

Life Changing Journey Series I and II

In Life Changing Journey - 365 Inspirational Quotes Series I, Shree Shambav curates a powerful collection of 365 original quotes across fourteen chapters, each crafted to touch the heart of our daily lives. More than a simple compilation, this series speaks directly to personal experiences with wisdom and depth. Quotes like, "The most beautiful things are unseen but can be felt," echo the quiet beauty of life's intangible moments. Another, "Giving up is easier; holding oneself up is wiser," provides a guiding light in challenging times. Life Changing Journey reveals the transformative power of carefully chosen words, inspiring readers to find strength and new perspectives on their paths. Through Shree Shambav's work, readers are reminded of the wisdom and resilience hidden within each day.

Twenty + One - 21 Short Stories Series I and II

In *Twenty + One - Short Stories*, Shree Shambav brings to life the often-overlooked characters of nature—trees, animals, and mountains—revealing their intrinsic worth beyond mere utility. With poetic personification, he gives voice to these silent beings, some of whom are lucky enough to have names, titles, and rare human protection. Mountains, usually seen as mere landmarks, are depicted with reverence, emphasising their enduring presence. The stories build a bridge between humans and the natural world, showing that pain, grief, and resilience are shared across all forms of life. Shambav invites readers to empathise with the silent struggles of trees and animals, inspiring a fresh perspective on ecology and our responsibility towards the environment. This collection is a call to honour our connection to nature, encouraging readers to foster compassion and respect for all life.

Learn To Love Yourself

Learn to Love Yourself is a powerful invitation to turn inward in a world focused on external validation and superficial measures. Through ten transformative chapters, each offering a key rule for self-love, readers are guided to uncover their inner beauty, cultivate personal strength, and develop a solid foundation of self-acceptance. This journey goes beyond momentary happiness; it's about building an authentic relationship with yourself that fosters resilience, joy, and fulfilment. From embracing your unique qualities and practising compassion to setting boundaries and pursuing what makes you come alive, this book provides essential insights and practical guidance. Let *Learn to Love Yourself* be your trusted companion on this path, inspiring you to unlock the limitless potential within and find true inner peace.

The Power of Letting Go

The Power of Letting Go invites you to release attachments, fears, and expectations, guiding you toward true inner freedom and joy. With deep insights, practical exercises, and timeless wisdom, this book equips you to face life's challenges with resilience and grace. It explores the essence of attachment, embraces the power of seven-year growth cycles, and teaches the art of forgiveness as a key to a fulfilled life. Each chapter brings concepts to life through relatable analogies and real stories, making profound ideas both accessible and engaging. Let this book serve as your beacon for self-discovery and spiritual awakening, helping you navigate uncertainties and unlock your potential for a joyful, meaningful existence.

A Journey of Lasting Peace

A Journey of Lasting Peace is a transformative guide to self-love, inner peace, and personal strength, where Shree Shambav leads readers through 18 powerful principles for discovering their true selves. Each chapter explores vital themes, from the quest for inner peace and the importance of self-awareness to the healing practices of mindfulness and yoga. Through practical strategies, reflective exercises, and heartfelt stories, this book offers a clear roadmap to a more authentic and fulfilling life.

Whether you seek to embrace imperfection, establish healthy boundaries, or reconnect with nature, A Journey of Lasting Peace provides the wisdom to navigate life's challenges and find enduring tranquillity. Perfect for anyone on a journey of self-discovery, this inspiring work gently reminds us that lasting peace starts within.

TWENTY + ONE

Astrology Unveiled: Series I and V

Astrology Unveiled: Foundations of Ancient Wisdom invites you to unlock the mysteries of astrology, offering timeless knowledge rooted in the teachings of ancient sages. This comprehensive guide explores fundamental principles like Rashi, Graha, Bhava, and Divisional charts, making it an essential resource for beginners and intermediate students alike.

With logical explanations and practical applications, Shree Shambav skilfully blends ancient insights with modern understanding. Rich in examples, detailed explanations, and engaging exercises, this book serves as an illuminating path to mastering Vedic astrology.

Embark on a transformative cosmic journey, discovering how astrology can unveil your destiny, guide life's choices, and support your spiritual growth.

The Entitlement Trap: Get Over It, Get On It

Are you feeling stuck in a cycle of blame and dissatisfaction? The Entitlement Trap: Get Over It, Get On It offers a transformative path to reclaiming your personal power. This insightful guide helps you break free from the mindset of victimhood and empowers you to take control of your life. Inside, you'll discover how to redefine success, prioritize your true values, and live with purpose. Through practical strategies, you'll learn to embrace simplicity, connect with nature, and leave a lasting legacy. Get ready to shift from powerless to empowered and create a life you love!

Whispers of a Dying Soul: Unspoken Regrets and Unlived Dreams

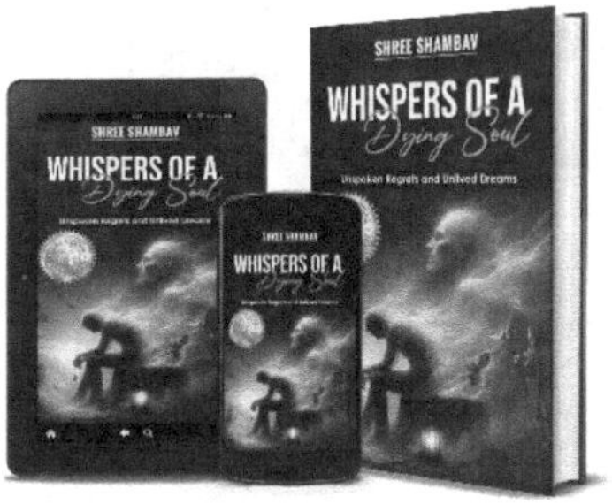

"Whispers of a Dying Soul", embarks on a profound journey that delves into the silent longings we often carry but seldom express. This powerful exploration uncovers the unspoken emotions that shape our lives—missed opportunities, unfulfilled dreams, and the quest for authenticity. Through heartfelt reflections and transformative insights, this book invites you to confront your regrets and turn them into powerful catalysts for growth and healing.

Whispers of the Soul: A Journey Through Haiku Series I to IV

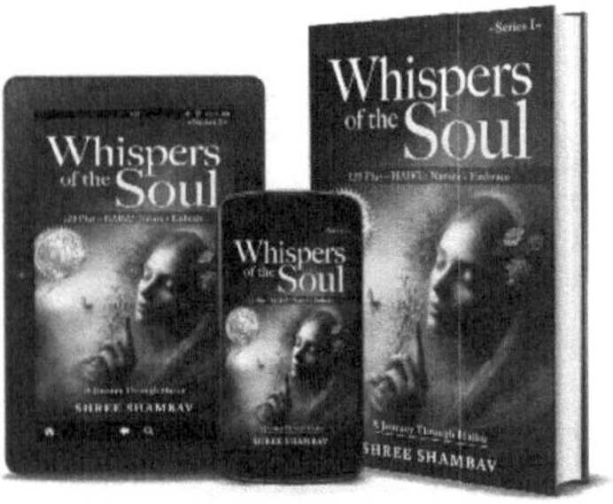

"Whispers of the Soul: A Journey Through Haiku" is a poetic invitation to pause and rediscover life's hidden beauty. This transformative collection of haikus explores themes of nature, mindfulness, love, and the human journey, offering profound reflections on universal experiences. Divided into five series, the book delves into nature's elegance, the depths of inner stillness, the tenderness of human connection, the passage of life's seasons, and the mysteries beyond the self. Each haiku captures fleeting moments with timeless grace, guiding readers toward peace, self-discovery, and a renewed appreciation for life's simplest wonders. This is more than poetry—it's a soulful journey.

The Power of Words: Transforming Speech, Transforming Lives

The Power of Words: Transforming Speech, Transforming Lives illuminates the profound influence of our everyday language. This book explores how words can heal or harm, connect or divide, urging readers to embrace mindful communication. It delves into the "Sins of Speaking," such as gossip and judgment, while celebrating virtues like honesty, kindness, and authenticity. With practical strategies for transformation and a focus on the art of listening, Shree Shambav offers a roadmap to elevate our conversations. Perfect for both personal growth and professional development, this guide inspires readers to use their words to create peace, foster deeper connections, and lead a life of integrity and purpose.

The Art of Intentional Living: Minimalism for a Life of Purpose

In a world that celebrates more, The Art of Intentional Living invites you to embrace less. This powerful guide explores how minimalism can transform every aspect of your life—your space, your time, and your mind—by removing distractions and focusing on what truly matters.

Through simple yet profound principles, you'll learn to:

- Declutter your physical and digital space
- Prioritise what aligns with your values
- Create time for meaningful connections and experiences
- Cultivate a life of purpose, peace, and clarity

Awakening the Infinite: The Power of Consciousness in Transforming Life

In a fragmented world, Awakening the Infinite explores the power of consciousness to heal, transform, and unite. This book takes you on an experiential journey, revealing how awareness shapes reality and connects us to universal wisdom. Through spiritual teachings, introspection, and practical insights, it helps you uncover your soul's true purpose. With transformative practices, it guide you toward emotional healing, clarity, and personal growth. As you deepen your awareness, you'll forge a profound connection with yourself and the world around you. Embracing this journey leads to a life of mindfulness, authenticity, and purpose. Ultimately, it is an invitation to awaken the infinite potential within.

Beyond the Veil: A Journey Through Life After Death

Discover the Eternal Mystery of Life After Death What happens when we die? Is it the end, or a transition to something greater? In Beyond the Veil: A Journey Through Life After Death, explore humanity's greatest mystery through the lens of science, spirituality, and philosophy.

From near-death experiences to ancient spiritual teachings, this transformative book bridges the gap between the physical and the infinite, offering profound insights into the afterlife. Whether you're seeking comfort, answers, or inspiration, this journey will deepen your understanding of life, death, and what lies beyond.

9 789334 263978

Printed at Repro India Ltd.